LORD OF THE
RINGS
& The Eucharist

by

Scott L. Smith, Jr.

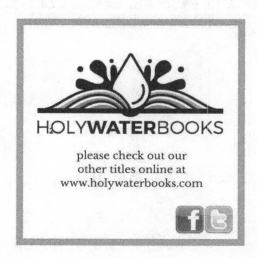

please check out our
other titles online at
www.holywaterbooks.com

Cover design by Holy Water Books

Out of the darkness of my life, so much frustrated, I put before you the one great thing to love on earth: *the Blessed Sacrament*. There you will find romance, glory, honour, fidelity, and the true way of all your loves on earth, and more than that: Death.

J.R.R. Tolkien.

Now
Also available as an
Audiobook
through Audible

Narrated by
Kevin O'Brien
who has portrayed
J.R.R. Tolkien
on stage and screen

Table of Contents

Table of Figures

LORD OF THE RINGS
&
THE EUCHARIST

WHAT DID TOLKIEN SAY ABOUT BEING CATHOLIC?

For a man living in an Anglican country, J.R.R. Tolkien didn't keep his cards too close to his chest. He was unabashedly Catholic. He lived in a country in which the king and queen were acknowledged as the heads of a church, which explicitly denied the authority of the pope. To this, Tolkien stated the following:

> I myself am convinced by the Petrine claims, nor looking around the world does there seem much doubt which is the True Church, the temple of the Spirit dying but living, corrupt but holy, self-reforming and re-arising.[1]

Moreover, the Thirty-Two Articles, upon which the Church of England was founded, admitted only of a symbolic presence of Christ in the Eucharist.

This error, according to Tolkien, was sufficient to invalidate the legitimacy of the Church of England. Conversely, the Blessed Sacrament proved the Petrine claims of the Catholic Church:

> But for me that Church of which the Pope is the acknowledged head on earth has as chief claim that it is the one that has ever defended the Blessed Sacrament, and given it most honour, and put in the prime place.

Figure 1: J.R.R. Tolkien (1892–1973)

Again, with respect to the Eucharist, he had little patience for the Protestant Reformation, which he described as a "revolt":

> "Feed my sheep" was His last charge to St. Peter; and since His words are always first to be understood literally, I suppose them to refer primarily to the Bread of Life. It was against this that the West European revolt was really launched – "the blasphemous fable of the Mass" – and faith works a mere red herring.[2]

This is an incredible statement from Tolkien, who was himself a daily communicant and encouraged such for his son elsewhere in the letter quoted above. The Anglican Church, in Article 31 of the 32 Articles mentioned above, describes the Real Presence of Christ in the Eucharist as "the blasphemous fable of the Mass." Amazingly, the father of the modern fable, himself, turns this on its head, mocking the Anglican Church.

In the following book, we will further explore the Eucharist's possible appearances in Tolkien's writing, as well as other Christian dogmas, whether uniquely Catholic or not.

Endnotes:

[1] *Tolkien: Man and Myth*, p. 193.
[2] *The Letters of J.R.R. Tolkien*, Letter 250, written to Michael Tolkien, November 1, 1963.

WHAT DID TOLKIEN SAY ABOUT THE EUCHARIST?

Tolkien's treatment of the Eucharist is amazingly thorough. Tolkien laid "bread crumbs," so to speak, for us to find the Eucharist hidden inside his writings. The key and starting point is the Lembas Bread.

Following the thread of the Lembas Bread will take us back to the beginning of Middle-Earth, to Tolkien's Eden where the Two Trees grew. The last surviving descendant of the Two Trees will take us to the end and climax of the story. The trees take us to the last surviving descendent of the Kingdom of Númenor and, ultimately, to the **Return of the King**.

This is the image worn by all the knights and kings of Gondor. It is of the tree and the crown. It might also remind you of the crown of twelve stars worn by the Blessed Virgin Mary in the Book of Revelation.

Figure 2: Tree of Gondor

Here are several quotes from Tolkien regarding the Eucharist.[3] Reading these, one begins to understand how significant the Eucharist was to Tolkien's thinking and, what's more, his imagining.

> Out of the darkness of my life, so much frustrated, I put before you the one great thing to love on earth: the Blessed Sacrament. There you will find romance, glory, honour, fidelity, and the true way of all your loves on earth, and more than that: Death.

> By the divine paradox, that which ends life, and demands the surrender of all, and yet by the taste—or foretaste—of which alone can what you seek in your earthly relationships (love, faithfulness, joy) be maintained, or take on that complexion of reality, of eternal endurance, which every man's heart desires.

How many of Tolkien's characters experience "sagging" faith and require almost "eternal endurance"? And what nourishes Sam and Frodo on their journey into darkness? The Eucharist, which is "the only cure":

> The only cure for sagging or fainting faith is Communion. Though always itself, perfect and complete and inviolate, the

Blessed Sacrament does not operate completely and once for all in any of us. Like the act of Faith it must be continuous and grow by exercise.

Tolkien also has words of wisdom for those, like so many of us, that complain of Mass being boring or full of distractions and so lose track of what really matters:

Frequency [of the Eucharist] is of the highest effect. [...]

Seven times a week is more nourishing than seven times at intervals. Also I can recommend this as an exercise (alas! only too easy to find opportunity for): make your Communion in circumstances that affront your taste. Choose a snuffling or gabbling priest or a proud and vulgar friar; and a church full of the usual bourgeois crowd, ill-behaved children—from those who yell to those products of Catholic schools who the moment the tabernacle is opened sit back and yawn—open-necked and dirty youths, women in trousers and often with hair both unkempt and uncovered. Go to Communion with them (and pray for them). [...]

It could not be worse than the mess of the feeding of the Five Thousand—after which our Lord propounded the feeding that was to come. [...]

It will be just the same (or better than that) as a mass said beautifully by a visibly holy man, and shared by a few devout and decorous people.

It is remarkable that such a literary giant as J. R. R. Tolkien should be so unabashedly Catholic. Now that I think about it, maybe Tolkien's devotion to the Eucharist just brings everything into focus ...

Endnote:

[3] *The Philosophy of Tolkien: The Worldview Behind* The Lord of the Rings, p. 219.

THE BREAD OF LIFE
& LEMBAS BREAD

This is how the Lady Galadriel described Lembas or Elven Waybread in the Common Tongue:

Eat little at a time, and only at need. For these things are given to serve you when all else fails. The cakes will keep sweet for many many days, if they are unbroken and left in their leaf-wrappings, as we have brought them. One will keep a traveler on his feet for a day of long labour, even if he be one of the tall men of Minas Tirith.[4]

You can hear echoes of Tolkien's own words in those of Lady Galadriel. One wafer, the Lady says, "will keep a traveler on his feet for a day of long labour."

Figure 3: Legolas holding the lembas in Fellowship of the Ring,
Copyright New Line Cinema

Or, as Tolkien wrote of the Eucharist, one "taste" provides for "eternal endurance" to reach that ultimate goal "which every man's heart desires." It will be described in a later section how Lady Galadriel is a symbol for Mary, and, as such, it is highly significant that she supplies the fellowship with Eucharistic bread.

Tolkien hints at the Eucharistic significance of the lembas bread. He wrote that the lembas "also has a much larger significance, of what one might hesitatingly call a 'religious' kind. This becomes later apparent especially in the chapter 'Mount Doom'."[5]

The Bread which Feeds theWill

Tolkien is likely referring to this "larger significance" in this passage from the chapter "Mount Doom":

> As for himself, though weary and under a shadow of fear, [Sam] still had some strength left. The lembas had a virtue without which they would long ago have lain down to die. It did not satisfy desire, and at times Sam's mind was filled with the memories of food, and the longing for simple bread and meats. And yet this waybread of the Elves had a potency that increased as travellers **relied on it alone** and did not mingle it with other foods. **It fed the will, and it gave strength to endure,** and to master sinew and limb beyond the measure of mortal kind.[6]

Relying on the lembas bread *alone* is reminiscent of the many saints, including Saint Catherine of Siena during the last years of her life, who survived by eating the Eucharist alone. Many of the saints survived on the Eucharist alone during the fasting seasons of Lent and Advent. St. Joseph Cupertino also lived on the Eucharist alone for five years.

The lembas is also described as "[feeding] the will" of Frodo and Sam, who are on the final leg of their journey to Mount Doom.[7] This strengthening of the will that comes from eating lembas is the effect of the Viaticum.

Bread from the Journey

The Viaticum is the Last Eucharist given to those who are dying. The *Catechism of the Council of Trent* says: "Sacred writers call it the Viaticum as well because it is the spiritual food by which we are supported in our mortal pilgrimage, as also because it prepares for us a passage to eternal glory and happiness."[8]

Viaticum is "bread for the journey" to the Promised Land. Lembas was the "bread for the journey" of Sam and Frodo to Mordor. Frodo bearing the great weight of the One Ring to Mount Doom is strikingly similar to Jesus bearing the weight of the Cross to Calvary. Frodo was sustained by the bread; Jesus was offering it as His Body.

Not only that, we are about to dig deep into the question: Where did the lembas bread come from? It was originally the bread for the greatest journey of Middle-Earth.

Receiving the Eucharist Unworthily

Lembas bread did not taste good to everyone. Remember Gollum's response to the lembas bread offered to him by Frodo and Sam? Why was this?

Let's look for a moment to the epistles of St. Paul, 1 Corinthians 11:27-30:

> Whoever, therefore, eats the bread or drinks the cup of the Lord in an **unworthy manner** will be guilty of profaning the body and blood of the Lord. Let a man examine himself, and so eat of the bread and drink of the cup. For anyone who eats and drinks without discerning the body eats and **drinks judgment upon himself**. That is why many of you are weak and ill, and some have died

St. Paul instructs us that is a grave matter to receive the Eucharist unworthily. This means mortal sin. If you receive the Eucharist without first confessing all of your mortal sins, you are guilty of "profaning the body and blood of the Lord." Not only that, you are drinking judgment upon yourself. Otherwise translated, you are drinking death upon yourself.

Gollum somehow knew this. Or, at least his taste buds did. Gollum refused outright to eat the lembas.[9]

Gollum was even repelled by the lembas bread. Gollum reacts violently in the movie version, if you remember the following scene:

Figure 4: The Two Towers, *Copyright New Line Cinema*

Does this mean Gollum was in a state of mortal sin? Of course, he was. Gollum had murdered his brother to take possession of the One Ring. Then, he had possessed the One Ring for centuries, drinking in its poison, growing mad, and doing unspeakable things in the dark beneath the Misty Mountains.

Gollum even betrays Frodo and Sam by *disposing* of the lembas bread. Catholic would never just throw bits of the Eucharist in the garbage. It must all be consumed or stored reverently in the tabernacle.

Cram

One last interesting detail about the lembas bread before we undertake the Great Journey to the Undying Lands.

The immortal Elves were not the only race of Middle-Earth to have a waybread. The Dwarves, too, had a counterpart to Lembas called "Cram".

There's a certain inelegance to the name "Cram". The name conjures up images of dwarves "cramming" the bread into their mouths without ceremony or backstory. The dwarves, too, were not immortal like the Elves.

One has to wonder about this. Was Tolkien remarking on the counterparts to the Eucharist in other non-Catholic Christian churches? Was Tolkien criticizing other Christian churches for rejecting the Real

Presence of Christ in the Eucharist? While the lembas is supernatural bread, perhaps cram is mere bread, good only for cramming into one's mouth.

Speaking of counterparts to the Eucharist, Tolkien may even deploy the imagery of a **"dark" Eucharist** with the Eye of Sauron. This disfiguring of the Eucharist shows us just how evil Sauron is. The Peter Jackson movies depict this very well. See the side-by-side below:

Endnotes:

[4] *The Fellowship of the Ring*, "Farewell to Lorien"

[5] *Letters*, p. 274-275, 1958.

[6] *The Return of the King*, Book Six, Chapter III, "Mount Doom"

[7] This is also seen as Aragorn, Gimli, and Legolas hunt the orc pack across the plains of Rohan: "Often in their hearts, they thanked the Lady of Lórien for the gift of lembas, for they could eat of it and find new strength even as they ran." (*The Two Towers*, Book Three, Chapter II, "The Riders of Rohan")

[8] De Euch. sacr., n. 3

[9] *The Lord of the Rings, The Return of the King*, Book Six, Chapter I: "The Tower of Cirith Ungol"

WHERE DID THE LEMBAS BREAD COME FROM?

Tolkien provides us with some of the bread's history elsewhere in his writing. It is interesting that Tolkien should dedicate so much time to writing about bread if he was not hinting at a greater significance to the bread.

We have discussed the basic connection between the Lembas Bread and the Eucharist, as well as J. R. R. Tolkien's devotion to the Eucharist. Now, let's follow Tolkien down the path a bit further: "it's a dangerous business, Frodo, going out your door. You step onto the road, and if you don't keep your feet, there's no knowing where you might be swept off to."

It is said by the Eldar that the art of preparing the Lembas came from the Valar Yavanna. Yavanna was one of the Ainu or the "Holy Ones." These were the first and mightiest of the beings created by Eru Ilúvatar, "the One", before the creation of the world. We will return to Eru Ilúvatar later in this book in our discussion of the Trinity in Tolkien's writings.

Yavanna

All growing things and fruits were attributed to Yavanna. In the Elvish language, Yavanna's name means "Giver of Fruits." Here are some artists' depictions of Yavanna:

Figure 5: Yavanna *by Ulla Thynell*

The art of preparing the lembas bread is said to have originated as far back as the Elves' Great Journey to Aman, when Yavanna brought to them a special corn grown on her own fields. These traditions were passed on throughout the long ages from house to house of the High Elves.

The Elves' Great Journey

This is very interesting. For what might Tolkien's "Great Journey" be an allegory?

The Great Journey was the march of the elves, the Eldar, from Cuiviénen, the place of their awakening, to Valinor. Valinor is elsewhere called the Undying Lands. Only immortals such as the elves and ringbearers are permitted to live in the Undying Lands. Valinor is, therefore, the equivalent of Heaven or the Promised Land.

Figure 6: The Exodus of the Israelites out of Egypt

When in salvation history was there a "great journey," or "Exodus", to the Promised Land? The Great Journey of the Eldar is an allegory for the Exodus of the Israelites out of Egypt. The Great Journey is the equivalent of the Wilderness Wanderings, the forty years the Israelites spent wandering in the desert and wilderness of the Sinai Peninsula.

But wait, what did the Israelites *eat* during those forty years spent wandering in the desert? Wasn't it some kind of *bread*?

The Manna

The Manna was the miraculous bread that fed the Israelites for forty years in the desert, cf. Exodus 16; Numbers 11:6-9. It was called bread from heaven. The Manna appeared daily, except on the Sabbath. This is the origin of the "daily bread" described in the Our Father.

The Manna fell during the night in small white flakes or grains which covered the ground and appeared as hoar frost. The Manna came down "like the dewfall" – does that sound familiar? This is part of the Eucharistic prayer said during the Mass. The Holy Spirit comes "like the dewfall".

God said to Moses, "I will rain down bread from heaven" (Ex 14:4). God then instructed Moses to tell the people of Israel, "In the morning, you shall have your fill of bread, so that you may know that I, the Lord, am your God" (Ex 14:12). The following morning, "when the **dew** evaporated," the people awoke and found the manna, "the bread which the Lord has given you to eat" (Ex 14:13-15).

The Manna is described as resembling coriander seed and bdellium, with a taste like "flour with honey" or "bread tempered with oil" (Exodus 16:31; Numbers 11:7-8).

The manna formed on the ground as flakes or wafers. Does that sound familiar? Bread in the shape of wafers? The manna is clearly a prefigurement of the Eucharist, the bread from heaven which becomes the flesh of Christ during the consecration during the Catholic Mass.

Jesus' followers actually ask him about the manna at the beginning of the Bread of Life discourse, John 6:30-31:

> Then what sign do you do, that we may see, and believe you? What work do you perform? Our fathers ate the manna in the wilderness; as it is written, 'He gave them bread from heaven to eat.'

This marks the beginning of Jesus' Bread of Life discourse. He declares that he, himself, is the "Bread of Life." Jesus' own flesh is the new Manna. The Eucharist is the fulfillment of the Manna.

If the origin of lembas bread wasn't enough, Tolkien makes even more connections between the lembas bread and the Eucharist. For example, he describes the lembas bread as a "wafer":

> 'Praised be the bow of Galadriel, and the hand and eye of Legolas!' said Gimli, as he munched a **wafer** of lembas. 'That was a mighty shot in the dark, my friend!'[10]

In the *History of Middle-Earth*, Tolkien also describes how, during the First Age, lembas was wrapped in "leaves of silver [...] a **wafer** of white wax shaped as a single flower of Telperion."[11] Again, the lembas bread is described as a wafer, but also a *white* wafer. Just like the Eucharist. But there's more, where did these "leaves of silver" come from and what is "Telperion"?

Figure 7: Behold the Lembas of God!

Endnotes:

[10] *The Fellowship of the Ring*, Book Two, Chapter IX, "The Great River"
[11] *The History of Middle Earth*, Vol. XII: The Peoples of Middle-earth, chapter XV: "Of Lembas"

THE TWO TREES OF LORD OF THE RINGS & THE GARDEN OF EDEN

You know about the "Two Towers" of *The Lord of the Rings*, but what about these "Two Trees"? Also, where else have we heard of two, very consequential trees? This will eventually take us to this tree, the White Tree of Gondor.

Recall Tolkien's description of the lembas as wrapped in "leaves of silver [...] a wafer of white wax shaped as a single flower of Telperion."

What, or *Who*, was Telperion?

Laurelin and Telperion: The Two Trees of Valinor and Eden

Figure 8: The Two Trees of Valinor *by Roger Garland*

The first sources of all light for the world of Middle Earth were two enormous lamps. There was a silver lamp in the north called Illuin. There was also a golden lamp in the south called Ormal.

Think about what Scripture says about "lamps" and "light." Psalms 119:105 says "Thy word is a lamp to my feet and a light to my path." At the dawn of Creation, as described at the beginning of John's Gospel, the Word made flesh is the light of the world:

In the beginning was the Word, and the Word was with God, and the Word was God. He was in the beginning with God; all things were made through him, and without him was not anything made that was made. In him was life, and the life was the light of men. **The light shines in the darkness**, and the darkness has not overcome it.

Lastly, Jesus says at John 8:12, "I am the light of the world; he who follows me will not walk in darkness, but will have the light of life."

Melkor and Ungoliant – Satan and the Serpent

The lamps of Middle-Earth were struck down and destroyed by Melkor with the aid of Ungoliant. Melkor's name means "He Who Arises in Might." Melkor was originally the most powerful of those created by Eru Ilúvatar, the Godhead.

Melkor is the equivalent of Lucifer in Tolkien's mythology. Just as the angel Lucifer fell from grace and became Satan, Melkor became Morgoth, the first Dark Lord. He was so powerful that even his servant was unbelievably powerful. You already know who Morgoth's servant was. Sauron.

Ungoliant was a massive spider, like Shelob. In fact, Ungoliant was the mother of Shelob. She was likely even the first spider. Her origins were said to be from the darkness itself. Being a creature of darkness, she hungered for the light, eventually seeking to devour all light. But … "the darkness has not overcome" the light, as in John's gospel.

It is no wonder that we later see Ungoliant's child, Shelob, drawn to the One Ring that was forged by Sauron, whose master was the former master of Shelob's mother. But Shelob fails to overcome the bearer of the One Ring, Frodo, who bears the light which "shines in the darkness."

In Scripture Satan is depicted as a serpent when he slithers into Eden. Tolkien instead depicts his Satan figure, Melkor, as accompanied by a creature of darkness, a spider instead of a serpent.

It should also be noted that the Hebrew word for Satan's manifestation in Genesis is *nahash*. This word is translated into the Greek as *leviathan*, which is a massive serpent, not unlike the massive spider Ungoliant. Further, the serpent of Genesis is later referred to, in Revelation 12, as a dragon, which are also highly significant in Tolkien's mythology.

Figure 9: Ungoliant and Melkor at the Two Trees by John Howe

Figure 10: The Temptation of Adam and Eve *by Michelangelo*

Ezellohar & Eden

Together Melkor-Morgoth and Ungoliant destroyed the lamps of light. Afterward, the Valar went to the Undying Lands. There, Yavanna hallowed a high, green place. There, she sang into being Two Trees to bear the light of the Two Lamps.

The Two Trees that grew in the Undying Lands were the silver Telperion and the golden Laurelin, male and female, respectively. The Trees sat on the green hill Ezellohar located outside Valimar, the city of the Valar.

Ezellohar translates as "Green Mound" and was also called Corollairë. It stood before the western gates of Valimar.[12] Not only was it hallowed by Yavanna, it was watered by the tears of Nienna.

The Two Trees of Ezellohar should immediately call to mind the Two Trees of Eden, namely the Tree of Knowledge of Good & Evil and the Tree of Life. Sometimes, we forget that Eden was an orchard with, not one, but two very important trees.

Ezellohar bears many other resemblances to Eden. Eden was not just a garden, nor even just a hallowed place, like Ezellohar. It was also a high place, as were all the sites on which covenants were made between God and man. Think of where the New Covenant was made by Christ. It began in the *upper* room at the Last Supper, continued with His prayers in the *Garden* of Gethsemane, and concluded on the Cross atop *Mount* Calvary.

How do we know that Eden was a hill or mountain? Scripture tells us at Genesis 2:10 that "a river flowed out of Eden to water the garden, and there it divided and became four rivers." Rivers flow down from high places; therefore, Eden was either a hill or a mountain. Likely, Eden was a mountain because it was mother to the four great rivers.

Also, as Eden was shut following the work of Satan, Ezellohar was blackened.[13] Melkor/Morgoth and Ungoliant were not finished wreaking destruction. They became jealous of the beauty of the Two Trees. More on that below.

Silver Leaves, Wafers, and Dew

Each tree was a source of light. You can see that Tolkien was not a dualist with a tree of light and a tree of darkness. Both gave light. Good and evil are not equally powerful. Light always conquers the dark.

Each tree was also a source of its own sort of light. Telperion's light was silver and Laurelin's was gold.

Telperion had dark leaves, which were *silver* on one side. Telperion's leaves were used to wrap the lembas bread of the Eldar: "leaves of silver [...] a wafer of white wax shaped as a single flower of Telperion."

Also, Telperion's dew was silvery and was collected as a source of water and of light. It was revered and collected by the Varda.[14]

This is likely another reference to the Manna. See, for example,

Exodus 16:13-14:

> In the evening quails came up and covered the camp; and in the morning **dew** lay round about the camp. And when the **dew** had gone up, there was on the face of the wilderness a fine, flake-like thing, fine as hoarfrost on the ground.

The manna formed on the ground like *dew*. As we discussed above, the bread came down "like the dewfall". These words are uttered by the priest at the epiclesis of the Catholic Mass, at the consecration of the bread. This is when the work of the Holy Spirit changes the bread into the flesh of Christ.

Telperion, the Male Tree & the Tree of Life

It is perhaps most interesting that Telperion is the male of the pair of trees. This may be the most interesting connection of all. Not only is the male-female complementarity significant in Scripture, of the Two Trees of Eden, one is also depicted as male.

Telperion is the silver tree below:

Figure 11: Telperion and Laurelin *by Quentin Champion*

At Genesis 3:22, we are told the reason that Adam and Eve have been banished from the Garden of Eden: "lest [man] put forth his hand and take also of the Tree of Life, and eat, and live forever."

Adam and Eve were banished from Eden, lest they eat freely of the Tree of Life. "At the east of the garden of Eden," Genesis also states, God "placed the cherubim, and a flaming sword which turned every way, to guard the way to the Tree of Life."

The Book of Revelation, which is in many ways the direct sequel to

Genesis, references the Tree of Life in several places. See, for example, Revelation 2:7:

> To him who conquers I will grant to eat of the Tree of Life, which is in the paradise of God.

At the end of time, men will again eat from the Tree of Life. This, they will do in Paradise and, thus, receive immortality. Again, at Genesis 22:1-2, it is written:

> Then he showed me the river of the water of life, bright as crystal, flowing from the throne of God and of the Lamb through the middle of the street of the city; also, on either side of the river, the Tree of Life with its twelve kinds of fruit, yielding its fruit each month; and the leaves of the tree were for the healing of the nations.

In summary, man was forbidden to eat of the Tree of Life and was banished from Eden to ensure this. Now, in Heaven, man is again allowed to eat of the Tree of Life. What is this Tree of Life that we are to eat of in Heaven? Or *Who*?

The Tree of Life is Christ. It is the Eucharist. This is why the lembas is wrapped in the silver leaves of Telperion and adorned with its flower: the lembas is a symbol for the Eucharist and is wrapped in the leaves and flowers of Tolkien's Tree of Life.

The Fate of the Two Trees

As stated above, Melkor destroyed the Two Lamps with Ungoliant's help. Unfortunately, Melkor was not finished destroying things.

Melkor became jealous of the beauty of the Two Trees and Ungoliant hungered after their great light. Again, Melkor enlisted the help of the giant spider.[15] Melkor struck the trees down, and the spider drank of the trees' light and life.

Yavanna and Nienna again sang and wept. However, they succeeded only in resurrecting Telperion's last flower and Laurelin's last fruit. Telperion's flower became the Sun and Laurelin's fruit became the Moon.

Ungoliant had nevertheless succeeded in poisoning the light of the Two Trees. Similarly, following Satan's poisonous lies, not only did Adam and Eve fall, but the whole of nature fell with them.

From then on, the *true* light of the Two Trees was said only to abide in the Silmarils, the legendary jewels forged by the Elves. The Silmarils are the namesake of the Tolkien book which contains all of this history of Middle-Earth, the Silmarillion:

Because of the Elves great love of Telperion, Yavanna made a second tree like unto it. This tree stood in the city of Tirion. In this city, two of the clans of the Eldar, the Vanyar and the Ñoldor, dwelt together. These two clans, however, would soon become estranged, not unlike Cain and Abel and later the clans of Cain and Seth.

The tree of Tirion was named Galathilion. It was identical to Telperion except that it bore no light of its own. A seedling of Galathilion was planted on the island of Tol Eressëa. This tree was named Celeborn, which name means "silver tree." You might remember that Galadriel's husband, the Lord of Lothlorien, was also named Celeborn:

Figure 12: Movie still of Celeborn, Copyright New Line Cinema

As a Marian figure, herself, it is interesting that Galadriel's husband is named after an heir to the trees of Eden or Ezellohar.

Later, in the Second Age, a seedling of Celeborn was planted on the island of the Númenoreans. The Númenoreans were also called the Men of Westernesse, because their island lay west across the sea. They would also become known as the Dúnedain, of which Aragorn was among the last survivors.

The seedling of Celeborn became Nimloth, the White Tree of Númenor. Nimloth, as we will later see, is Tolkien's symbol, not just for the Kingdom of Númenor, but for the Kingdom of *Israel*, as well.

Nimloth survived through most of the reign of the Númenoreans. That is, until the rise of Sauron. Sauron took control of Númenor and made King Ar-Pharazôn chop down Nimloth. The wood of the tree was then burnt on the altars.

Despite Sauron's despoiling of the tree, Isildur managed to save a single fruit of Nimloth. Isildur suffered many wounds in his mission to rescue the tree and came near to death. When the first leaf opened in the spring, however, Isildur was miraculously healed of his wounds.

Remember Isildur? Isildur was the King of Gondor who picked up his father's sword, Narsil, and cut the One Ring from the hand of Sauron, himself.

Figure 13: Mural in Rivendell, depicting Isildur's defeat of Sauron,
Copyright New Line Cinema

Unable to destroy the evil ring, Isildur became a ringbearer and was ultimately destroyed by its evil. Isildur's downfall led to a gradual decay of the Kingdom of Gondor. Eventually, the line of kings was even broken, awaiting Isildur's heir and the Return of the King.

Before his downfall, Isildur was a great hero, saving a fruit from Nimloth, healing miraculously, and defeating the giant Sauron. Does this remind you of any Biblical king in particular?

One last thing, from the rescued fruit of Nimloth later came the White Tree of Gondor.

At last! We arrive at the White Tree of Gondor.

Endnotes:

[12] J.R.R. Tolkien, Christopher Tolkien (ed.), The Silmarillion, "Quenta Silmarillion: Of the Beginning of Days"

[13] J.R.R. Tolkien, Christopher Tolkien (ed.), *The Silmarillion*, "Quenta Silmarillion: Of the Darkening of Valinor"

[14] *The Silmarillion*, Quenta Silmarillion, Chapter I: "Of the Beginning of Days"

[15] *The Silmarillion*, Quenta Silmarillion, Chapter VIII: "Of the Darkening of Valinor"

THE RETURN OF THE KINGS: THE KINGDOMS OF GONDOR & ISRAEL

Do you remember the White Tree of Gondor?

It was the symbol of Gondor. Faramir and the knights of Gondor wore the tree on their armor, their breastplates, and shields:

Figure 14: Copyright New Line Cinema

The White Tree grew in the uppermost courtyard of the citadel of Minas Tirith:

Figure 15: The withered white tree in the citadel of Minas Tirith, Copyright New Line Cinema

The White Tree had withered in the years of the Stewards of Gondor, when the throne of Gondor was empty and there was no king.

The White Tree mysteriously bloomed again at the Return of the King:

But why? What is the significance of the blooming of this tree?

The White Tree of Gondor
& the Stump of Jesse

As Jesus was leaving Jericho, a voice rose from the crowd. It was Bartimaeus, the blind beggar. He was sitting in the dust, along the roadside. The blind man cried out, "Jesus, Son of David, have mercy on me!" (Mark 10:47) The blind man was screaming, groping around in his private darkness and among the cruel feet of the road. Why had this blind man called Jesus the Son of David? What did the blind man *see*?

The great prophet, Jeremiah, announced the coming of the Son of David:

> Behold, the days are coming, says the Lord, when I will raise up for David **a righteous Branch**, and he shall reign as king and deal wisely, and shall execute justice and righteousness in the land. In his days Judah will be saved, and Israel will dwell securely. And this is the name by which he will be called: 'The Lord is our righteousness.'

Jesus would be the son of David, i.e. a descendant of David, according to the flesh, according to Romans 1:3. This is why we are given the genealogy of Jesus at the beginning of Mathew's Gospel. But what of this "righteous Branch"?

The great prophet, Isaiah, also had something to say about this "branch":

> There shall come forth **a shoot from the stump of Jesse,** and **a branch shall grow out of his roots**. And the Spirit of the Lord shall rest upon him, the spirit of wisdom and understanding, the spirit of counsel and might, the spirit of knowledge and the fear of the Lord. And his delight shall be in the fear of the Lord.

The "stump of Jesse"? What is that and who is Jesse? Jesse is David's father. The tree that grew from Jesse was David and the lines of kings which succeeded him. When the line of kings was broken, the tree was cut down, leaving only a stump. Sound familiar?

Remember Bilbo's prophecy sung at the Council of Elrond:

> All that is gold does not glitter,
> Not all those who wander are lost;
> The old that is strong does not wither,
> **Deep roots** are not reached by the frost.
> From the ashes a fire shall be woken,
> A light from the shadows shall spring;
> Renewed shall be blade that was broken:
> **The crownless again shall be king.**[16]

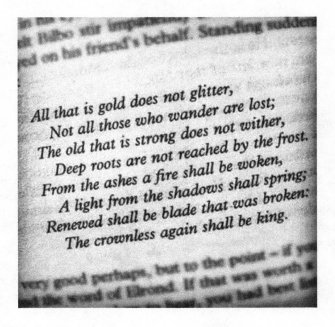

Isildur's Heir & the Son of David

Note the association of the heir to a broken line of kings, an ancient tree presumed dead, and the tree suddenly putting forth new growth, "a shoot" or "a branch".

Jesus is the Son of David, his descendant. He is heir to David's kingdom as the new King of Israel. Aragorn is Isildur's heir as the new King of Gondor. After so long without a king, the coming of Jesus and the coming of Aragorn marks the "Return of the King."

Figure 16: The White Tree *by Ted Nasmith*

The original White Tree of Gondor was made in the image of Telperion, the elder of the Two Trees of Valinor. The First White Tree of Gondor was the seed of Nimloth the Fair of Númenor, which was the seed of Celeborn of Tol Eressëa, which was the seed of Galathilion, which was the seed of Telperion.

Does the genealogy of the tree remind you of something?

The First White Tree of Minas Ithil was planted by Isildur in the Second Age. The Second White Tree was planted in Minas Anor by Isildur in the second year of the Third Age and lived 1,634 years.

The Third White Tree was planted by King Tarondor in Minas Tirith and lived for 1,212 years before dying under the rule of the Stewards. Since no seedling could be found, it was left standing as dead wood.

After being crowned king, Aragorn II discovers with Gandalf's help a sapling of the White Tree growing upon the slopes of Mindolluin, high above Minas Tirith. This, the king reverently plants in the place where the Third White Tree so long stood.

After standing dead for over 150 years, the Third White Tree is placed in the Tombs of the Kings, honored as though it were a monarch.

Genealogies

The genealogy of the White Tree reads much like the genealogy of Jesus, which is recited at the beginning of the Gospel of Matthew and again in Luke 3. This makes sense because the tree was so closely linked to the line of kings as to be a king, itself – the Third White Tree was even buried as a king!

The genealogy of Christ is evenly recited in Matthew in fourteen-generation sequences: "So all the generations from Abraham to David were fourteen generations, and from David to the deportation to Babylon fourteen generations, and from the deportation to Babylon to the Christ fourteen generations" (Matthew 1:17).

This genealogy demonstrates that Jesus is, literally, the Son of David. Similarly, the dynasty of the White Tree connects Isildur to Aragorn.

Remember, there are two genealogies of Jesus. While Mathew's genealogy focuses on Jesus being the Son of David, Luke's genealogy traces Jesus all the way back to God, through Adam, so as to describe Jesus as the New Adam. Similarly, the genealogy of the White Tree goes all the way back to Telperion, one of the Two Trees of Tolkien's Garden of Eden, which were divinely created similar to Adam.

King Isildur & King David

Lastly, even without these connections between Isildur and King David, i.e. heirship and the new growth of ancient trees, the two are still very much alike, both in their epic successes and their epic failures.

Sauron was decimating the armies of the Last Alliance of Elves and Men. Sauron towered above even Elendil the Tall, the first High King of Gondor and the greatest warrior of all the Dúnedain. Sauron had just killed not only the High King Elendil but the Elven-King Gil-galad, *and* he had shattered Elendil's sword. At this supreme moment, Isildur took up his father's broken sword and cut the One Ring from Sauron's hand.

Call me crazy, but ... Doesn't the slaying of the giant Sauron mirror David's slaying of the giant Goliath?

Figure 17: Isildur slaying the Giant, Sauron, Copyright New Line Cinema

Figure 18: David slaying the Giant, Goliath

Tragic Sins

There's more! Both Isildur and David were tempted and both committed massive, seemingly irredeemable, sins. These sins also eventually destroyed both their kingdoms.

Isildur turned back from casting the One Ring into the fires of Mount Doom. David turned back to Bathsheba bathing nude on the rooftop. Both of these sins crippled their effectiveness as rulers and rippled through their dynasties, as well.

Figure 19: Isildur becoming entranced by the One Ring,
Fellowship of the Ring, *Copyright New Line Cinema*

There is one last connection to mention, especially since it will introduce the next section. Again, we turn to the genealogies, but ascendants this time instead of descendants.

Isildur's father, Elendil, was the first High King of Gondor. He ruled over both the northern kingdom of Arnor and the southern kingdom of Gondor, as well as all the remaining Númenoreans, the Dúnedain.

King David, too, was the successor to the first High King. King David succeeded King Saul, the first king of a unified Israel. Later and in part due to David's sin, Israel would split into the Northern and Southern Kingdoms.

The Kingdom of Gondor
& The Kingdom of Israel

Originally there were two great kingdoms of Men, the Northern and Southern Kingdoms of Arnor and Gondor, respectively. The Northern Kingdom of Arnor never really recovered from a great war against the Morgoth, the evil Lord to which Sauron was only a lieutenant.

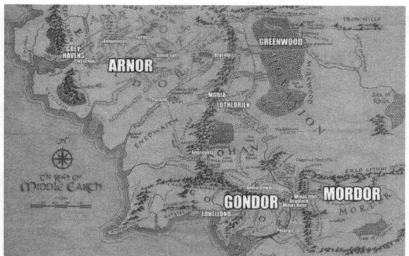

Figure 20: Map of the Northern and Southern Kingdoms of Men in Middle-Earth

Similarly, the Kingdom of Israel divided into the Northern and Southern Kingdoms around 1000 BC because of internal strife.

Ten of the Twelve Tribes of Israel formed the Northern Kingdom, called Israel. The remaining two tribes, Judah and Benjamin, formed the Southern Kingdom, called Judah. The northern tribes refused to accept Rehoboam, the son of Solomon, as their king.

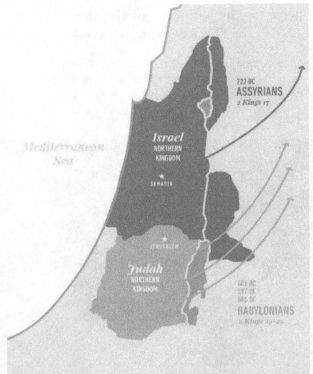

Figure 21: Map of the Northern and Southern Kingdoms of Israel

Isn't it amazing how similar these two maps are?

Both are bounded on the west by great seas: the Belegaer, which means "great sea", and the Mediterranean, respectively. Both kingdoms are also bounded on the east and connected by great rivers: the Anduin and the Jordan River, respectively.

As stated above, Kings Elendil and Isildur were the first two kings of a unified Kingdom of the Dúnedain, including both Gondor and Arnor. Similarly, Kings Saul and David were the first two kings of a unified Israel.

The kings that followed both Isildur and David, Valandil and Solomon, respectively, marked the end of the unified kingdoms.

Isildur and his three oldest sons were all killed at the Battle of the Gladden Fields. Only Valandil survived. Neither he nor his heirs ever claimed the throne of Gondor, despite keeping the title High King.

Absalom, though only the king's third son was David's favorite. Perhaps repeating the sins of his father, David's firstborn son Amnon raped Absalom's daughter, Tamar. Absalom eventually avenged his daughter by sending his servants to kill a drunken Amnon.

David's family situation quickly deteriorated from here. Despite being

David's favorite son, Absalom eventually rebelled against his father. In an interesting sidenote, which is addressed in greater depth elsewhere in this book, Absalom's death was the inspiration for the Ents, via Shakespeare (*see* the "Theology of the Ents"). More about trees!

Figure 22: The Death of Absalom, hanging from a tree

Following Absalom's death, Solomon became king and ruled over something of a golden age for the unified Israel. Nevertheless, it could not last. Solomon's successor Rehoboam dealt tactlessly with the economic complaints of the northern tribes, and around 930BC the kingdom split into two.

Arnor, the northern kingdom of Middle-Earth, eventually fell into a series of dynastic squabbles and petty wars. The Witch-King of Angmar, Sauron's second-in-command, eventually took over the entire region and ruled it for nearly a thousand years.

By the time of *The Hobbit*, all that remained of the once-great Kingdom of Arnor was the lands of the Hobbits, the village of men in Bree, and the nomadic remnant of the Dúnedain, known as the Rangers of the North. Isildur's heir, the prophesied king, will come from this remnant.

Similarly, the Northern Kingdom of Israel was ransacked by greater kingdoms, including the Assyrian Empire, and despoiled. The ten tribes which constituted the Northern Kingdom became known as the Lost Tribes of Israel. These tribes were scattered across the Mediterranean world, beginning the Jewish diaspora.

By the time of Jesus, all that remained of the Northern Kingdom were

small, scattered villages around the Sea of Galilee, like
... Nazareth. The heir to the throne of King David, the prophesied
Messiah, will come from this remnant.

What Good Can Come from the North?

Since both the Northern Kingdoms of Israel and Arnor were ransacked and destroyed, it is unthinkable that kings would come from there to restore the grandeur of the unified kingdoms.

Remember Boromir's words to Aragorn at the Council of Elrond in the movie adaptation: "*This* is Isildur's heir? A *ranger* from the *north? ...* Gondor needs no king." Boromir's quote from the book might be just as direct:

> 'And who are you, and what have you to do with Minas Tirith?'
> asked Boromir, looking in wonder at the lean face of the Ranger
> and his weather-stained cloak.[17]

Compare Boromir's rebuke to Nathanael's words at John 1: "What good can come from Nazareth?"

Phillip, one of Jesus' disciples, came to Nathanael and said to him, "We have found him of whom Moses in the law and also the prophets wrote, Jesus of Nazareth, the son of Joseph" (John 1:45). Nathanael said to him, *"Can anything good come out of Nazareth?"*

This is an amazing sidenote. Guess what "Nazareth" means in Hebrew? "Nazareth" comes from the Hebrew word *netser*, which literally means "place of the branch." This is the fulfillment of Isaiah's and Jeremiah's prophesies that a "branch" will grow from the "stump of Jesse".

Also, recall Isaiah's prophesy of the "Suffering Servant":

He was despised and rejected by men; a man of sorrows, and acquainted with grief; and as one from whom men hide their faces he was despised, and we esteemed him not. (Isaiah 53:3)

Compare this with Aragorn's description of his life before arriving in Rivendell and joining the Fellowship of the Ring:

Travellers scowl at us, and countrymen give us scornful names. "Strider" I am to one fat man who lives within a day's march of foes that would freeze his heart or lay his little town in ruin, if he were not guarded ceaselessly. Yet we would not have it otherwise. If simple folk are free from care and fear, simple they will be, and we must be secret to keep them so. That has been the task of my kindred, while the years have lengthened and the grass has grown.[18]

Bread for the Journey

That was quite a journey that the Lembas Bread took us along. It must seem obvious now how Tolkien infused his writing with great Biblical significance.

Let's go over the points one more time to recap:

- **Supernatural Bread for the Journey**: The lembas bread is waybread or bread for the journey. It provides supernatural strength to the will, sustaining the Fellowship on its long journey. Tolkien even describes its "much larger significance" and "of the religious kind".

- **Manna**: The lembas bread originated in the Elves Great Journey to the Undying Lands. Similarly, the roots of the Eucharist are the manna, which was the supernatural bread from heaven given by God to feed the Israelites in their Exodus from Egypt and Wilderness wanderings.

- **Eden**: The lembas bread traces back to Telperion, one of the two great trees of Tolkien's Eden, which was destroyed by Morgoth and Ungoliant. Likewise, the Eucharist is the fruit of Tree of Life of Eden. Man was cast out of Eden by the dragon-devil, the equivalent of Morgoth and Ungoliant.

- **Tree Prophecies**: The Kingdom of Númenor and Gondor-Arnor is represented by a genealogy of trees. The Tree of Gondor is dead, but it will bloom again at the return of the king. The Kingdom of Israel is represented as the Tree of Jesse. "A branch" will shoot forth from the "stump of Jesse" and a king will restore the kingdom.

- **Isildur-David**: King Isildur and King David are both giant killers of Sauron and Goliath, respectively. They both embrace in a tragic sin which ultimately destroys their kingdoms: not destroying the One Ring and the rape of Bathsheba, respectively.

- **Geography**: The kingdom of Númenor is split between the northern kingdom of Arnor and the southern kingdom of Gondor. The kingdom of Israel is split between the northern kingdom of Israel and the southern kingdom of Judah. In both, the northern kingdom falls, but is ultimately where the king is from. Both are also bound and connected on the west by great seas, Belegaer and the Mediterranean, and on the east by great rivers, Anduin and the Jordan.

Endnotes:

[12] J.R.R. Tolkien, Christopher Tolkien (ed.), The Silmarillion, "Quenta Silmarillion: Of the Beginning of Days"

[13] J.R.R. Tolkien, Christopher Tolkien (ed.), *The Silmarillion*, "Quenta Silmarillion: Of the Darkening of Valinor"

[14] *The Silmarillion*, Quenta Silmarillion, Chapter I: "Of the Beginning of Days"

[15] *The Silmarillion*, Quenta Silmarillion, Chapter VIII: "Of the Darkening of Valinor"

[16] *The Fellowship of the Ring*, Book Two, Chapter II, "The Council of Elrond"

[17] *The Fellowship of the Ring*, Book Two, Chapter II, "The Council of Elrond"

[18] Ibid.

THE CATHOLIC
THEOLOGY OF
THE LORD
OF THE RINGS

IS THE LORD OF THE RINGS CHRISTIAN ALLEGORY?

The worlds that J. R. R. Tolkien, the author of *Lord of the Rings*, created are nearly bottomless. Since the *Lord of the Rings* books were first published between 1954 and 1955, Tolkien was endlessly questioned about the symbolic meaning of the various characters. Did the War of the Ring represent World War II? Was the Dark Lord Sauron supposed to represent Hitler? Despite all this, Tolkien consistently denied writing an allegory.

As discussed in the previous section of this book, Tolkien's literary critics were too narrowly focused or perhaps too secular to see the obvious Eucharistic meaning of his work.

Nevertheless, in a letter to Stanley Unwin dated October 13, 1938, Tolkien derided any critic seeking allegory in his work. Even in the early stages of writing *Lord of the Rings*, he wrote "it [*Lord of the Rings*] is not an 'allegory'."[19]

Tolkien never sought out to write an allegory. He believed that an author who begins with the intention of writing an allegory has already failed. However, Tolkien also believed, almost paradoxically, that the closer he got to the truth in storytelling, the closer he came to a consistent allegory. "Allegory and Story," Tolkien wrote, "[converge] somewhere in Truth."[20]

So where does that leave us? Apart from the Eucharist and Biblical history, allegory and symbols were not intended by Tolkien. The War of the

Ring is not an allegory of the World Wars. Sauron is not Hitler. The One Ring is not the nuclear bomb or other instrument of war. These ideas doubtless influenced his writing, but were not direct symbols, but merely indirect. Tolkien's direct symbols, however, were reserved for the Eucharist and other Christian elements, as will be described below.

Endnotes:

[19] Carpenter, Humphrey, ed. *The Letters of J.R.R. Tolkien.* 1st ed. Massachusetts: George Allen & Unwin, 1981, 41.

[20] Ibid., 121.

THE TRINITY OF THE LORD OF THE RINGS

God the Father

Eru Ilúvatar is the Godhead of the Tolkien mythos. He is God the Father, the first person of the Trinity. The name, *Eru Ilúvatar*, means "The One" (Eru) and "Father of All" (Ilúvatar) in the ancient Elvish language of Quenya. You can make a direct connection between *Eru* and *El*, the word for God or "The One" in Hebrew, such as in *Elohim* ("the all-powerful One"), *El Shaddai* ("God Almighty"), *Gabriel* [Gabri-El] ("Strength of God"), and *Michael* [Micha-El] ("Who is like God?").

Gandalf and the other wizards and Maiar were born of the *thoughts* of Eru Ilúvatar (of God, the Father). Similarly, God the Father speaks the Word, which is the Son of God--the Word made Flesh is Jesus Christ. You might be thinking, "Tolkien's Trinity is way more than three persons."

Tolkien actually addressed all the gods, sub-gods, and co-gods in his mythology. In a draft letter to Peter Hastings, the manager of a Catholic bookshop in Oxford, Tolkien explained his mix of monotheism and polytheism and its seeming unorthodoxy. All these gods are "a tribute to the infinity of [God's] potential variety."[21] A creature, Tolkien argued, does not necessarily have to create in the same manner as he was created.

However, there are powers reserved to Eru Ilúvatar alone, such as the power of RESURRECTION, and other interventions into the natural order. And so, God the Son incarnated as Jesus was revealing something particular about his Divine Nature and the Christian Trinity when he said, "I am the Resurrection and the life" (Jn 11:25). Gandalf, unlike Jesus, did not share in the Divine Nature of Eru Ilúvatar. Gandalf, unlike Jesus, did not resurrect himself.

Gandalf as Christ: The Resurrection

Have you ever noticed how similar Gandalf's death and resurrection are to Christ's? Let's take a moment to walk through the events immediately preceding Gandalf the Grey's resurrection as Gandalf the White.

Figure 23: The return of Gandalf, Copyright New Line Cinema

Who is Gandalf?

Gandalf is one of the five Istari or Wizards sent to Middle-earth by the Valar in the Third Age. Galdalf is the wisest of the Maiar, who are minor Ainu. The Ainu, which means "Holy Ones," were the first of the creations of Eru Ilúvatar. The Maiar were born of his thought.

This is very much like the Word of God, which is made flesh. The wizards – Gandalf, Saruman, Radagast, et al. – were each a Maiar, and existed before Elves, Men, and Dwarves.

How Old is Gandalf?

Gandalf states that "300 lives of men, I have walked this earth." Taking the average life expectancy of man, conservatively, at 50, that would put Gandalf at the ripe old age of 15,000. That's fifteen *thousand* years old!

After 15,000 long years, Gandalf is about to die ...

Figure 24: Gandalf confronts the Balrog at the Bridge of Kazad-dûm

The trouble began when Gandalf was forced to finally confront the Balrog of Morgoth on the Bridge of Kazad-dûm. The Balrog had pursued the Fellowship throughout the mines of Moria and would have, presumably, pursued them beyond the Dimrill (eastern) gate of Moria, as well.

> Suddenly Frodo saw before him a black chasm. At the end of the hall, the floor vanished and fell to an unknown depth. The outer door could only be reached by a slender bridge of stone, without kerb or rail, that spanned the chasm with one curving spring of fifty feet. They could only pass across it single file. At the brink Gandalf halted and the others came up in a pack behind.[22]

Gandalf turned and confronted the Balrog, wielding the "Secret Fire," which will be discussed in the next section.

Gandalf blocks the narrow bridge, allowing the others to escape. Gandalf shatters the Balrog's sword and then cracks the bridge with his staff. The wizard ultimately defeats the Balrog on the bridge, but in so doing seals his own fate, as well. They both fall from the bridge together.

Together, the Balrog and the wizard fall down into the deepest hole beneath Middle Earth. They fall and they fall and the *fall*. They fell for a very long time, possibly hours to even an entire day. All the while, Gandalf was burning in the Balrog's fire.

At the end of the nearly endless descent, they plunge together into the deep lake beneath the roots of the mountain. Gandalf would later call this lake as cold as the tide of death and that it nearly froze his heart.

Gandalf and the Balrog fought in the lake until the creature fled into the dark tunnels which surround the lake. Gandalf describes these tunnels as hiding dark secrets:

> Far, far below the deepest delving of the Dwarves, the world is gnawed by nameless things. Even Sauron knows them not. They are older than he. Now I have walked there, but I will bring no report to darken the light of day.[23]

One of these "nameless things" might even have been the Watcher in the Water that hid at the entrance of the western gate of Moria.

Gandalf pursued the creature farther until the Balrog led him to the Endless Stair. Following the Balrog was Gandalf's only means of escaping the pit. The Endless Stair spiraled up from the roots of the mountain all the way the pinnacle of the Silvertine above the clouds.

The stair led to Durin's Tower in the living rock of Zirakzigil. The Balrog likely learned the way to Durin's Tower from Durin, himself, as the Balrog was named "Durin's Bane".

They fought on the highest peak of the highest mountain until at last Gandalf threw down his enemy. So massive was Gandalf's adversary that it broke the mountain-side as it fell.

After his victory, darkness took Gandalf, and he died. His body lay on the peak as on a giant altar. The entire battle, from Bridge of Khazad-dûm to the mutual demise of Gandalf and the Balrog, took ten days.

So, how does Christ's victory over Satan on the Cross resemble a wizard fighting a demon? Further, how does Christ's descent into Hell, Resurrection, and eventual Ascension compare with Gandalf's great fall into the depths and rising again?

Gandalf Casts Down the Power of Evil, Just as Christ Defeated Satan's Power Over Death on the Cross

Balrog is basically a demon. It is a Balrog created by Morgoth, formerly named Melkor. This is the Satan figure in *The Lord of the Rings*. Sauron once fought alongside Morgoth as his lieutenant.

Gandalf is a Sacrificial Lamb, Just as Christ is the Lamb of God

Gandalf lays down his life for the Fellowship. He is the sacrificial lamb. In ancient Jewish tradition, all the sin of the nation was heaped onto the back of a lamb or goat.

The goat was the "scape-goat". This is where that term originated. The goat was then thrown off a cliff as a sacrifice. In much the same way, Gandalf sacrifices himself willingly (the goat wasn't a willing sacrifice) to save the Fellowship. But it is the power of sin and evil, the Balrog, that casts Gandalf over the edge of the precipice.

Gandalf Wields a Sword, Just as Christ Wields the Sword of Truth

Gandalf's sword breaks the Balrog's sword. Gandalf wields Glamdring, a legendary sword. Though Gandalf found Glamdring in a troll-hoard along with Bilbo's sword Sting in *The Hobbit*.

The history of this sword traces back over 6,500 years. Glamdring was originally wielded by Turgon, the King of Gondolin. At the hand of Turgon, the sword earned the name "Foe-Hammer."

Figure 25: Gandalf and Glamdring, Copyright New Line Cinema

The armor of God is described at Ephesians 6:16-17: "Above all taking the shield of faith, with which you can quench all the flaming darts of the evil one. And take the helmet of salvation, and the sword of the Spirit, which is the word of God."

When Gandalf stands alone before the Balrog, he is clearly wielding faith, the shield of Scripture. More direct than that, he is the wielder of the Secret Fire, which is the Holy Spirit in the Tolkien universe. Gandalf is, therefore, wielding the Sword of the Spirit.

Gandalf and Christ Both Begin Their Descent into the Depths from a Cross

When Gandalf strikes his staff against the narrow bridge of Khazad-dûm, the wizard's staff and the bridge together form a cross. Even Gandalf's wooden staff, itself, is a sort of cross. It is very much like a bishop's crozier or staff, most of which are cross-shaped.

Here is an example of Pope St. John Paul the Great, the Bishop of Rome, wielding his crozier:

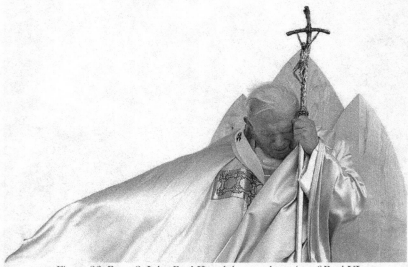

Figure 26: Pope St John Paul II and the papal crozier of Paul VI

Gandalf's Victory over Evil Results in His Death, Just like Christ

Genesis 3:15 is called the Proto-Evangelium or "first Gospel," because it describes the events of the Gospel in detail, including the Immaculate Conception, the Virgin Birth, and Christ's Passion and Death. At Genesis 3:15 God states that the Messiah "shall bruise [the serpent's] head," but in so doing, the serpent "shall bruise his heel."

In Christ's Passion and Death, he strikes at the serpent's skull. On the literal level, the Cross of Christ stabs into the ground at Golgotha, the "place of the skull."

The Cross of Christ also dealt a mortal blow to the skull of Satan, breaking his power over death. Even so, Christ accomplished these great works through his own death. That is, Satan struck out, like a serpent, biting Christ's heel. Christ and Satan mortally wound each other.

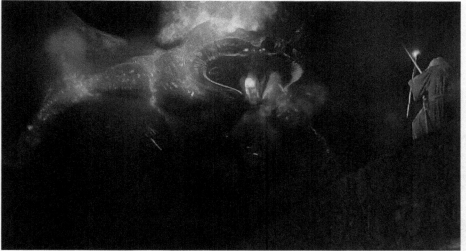

Figure 27: Gandalf confronts the Balrog at the Bridge of Kazad-dûm, Copyright of New Line Cinema

Similarly, Gandalf casts the Balrog into the abyss. In the midst of the wizard's triumph, however, the Balrog's whip lashes out *at Gandalf's heel* and they fall together into the abyss. The Balrog striking at Gandalf's *heel* cannot be a coincidence. Though there is also the possibility of an allusion to Achilles' infamous weakness, his heel, this is clearly a Messianic reference.

Though Gandalf and the Balrog cast each other into the abyss, they do not mortally wound each other, which is the "crux" of the Messianic symbolism. This happens later.

Gandalf pursues the Balrog down into the deepest depths and up to the highest peak. Thereupon, Gandalf smites the Balrog against the mountainside. Gandalf kills the Balrog and then shortly thereafter succumbs to death, himself. In the end, they mortally wound each other, just like Christ and Satan. There will be no resurrection for Satan and the Balrog, however.

Gandalf Descends into the Abyss, Just as Christ Descended into Hell

It can be no coincidence that Gandalf fell into the abyss after sacrificing himself. Immediately after his death on the cross, Christ descended into the abyss to hell.

Figure 28: Gandalf and Balrog by John Howe

The Apostles' Creed states that Christ "descended into hell" following his death on the cross. This is also called the "Harrowing of Hell." Christ didn't exactly descend into hell. It was more likely Sheol, the place where the dead, some righteous and some not, waited for the coming of the Messiah. In 1 Peter 3:19-20, we are given more information about where

Christ descended:

> [Jesus] went and preached to the spirits in prison, who formerly
> did not obey, when God's patience waited in the days of Noah,
> during the building of the ark, in which a few, that is, eight
> persons, were saved through water.

It is worth noting that a giant lake of water lay at the bottom of the
abyss in Lord of the Kings, as the verse above just happens to mention the
water of Noah's flood.

Gandalf Descends to "Hell" First through Fire and Then Through Cold, Similar to Dante's Depiction

When we think of hell, we often associate it with hellfire. Gandalf
definitely encounters fire in his descent, as he is burned all the way down
in the fire of the Balrog. Though Gandalf burns in the Balrog's fire, he is
not consumed. In this, he is like the Burning Bush which Moses
encountered in the desert. The ancient Hebrews also recognized the
burning bush as a type for the coming Messiah.

At the bottom of the almost bottomless abyss, however, is not a pool
of fire, but a bitterly cold lake. Gandalf would later call this lake as cold as
the tide of death and that it nearly froze his heart.

Compare this to the description of the Ninth Circle of Hell in Dante's
Inferno. At the center of the Ninth Circle is Satan himself frozen up to his
breast in ice. The beating of Satan's wings creates the ice which ensnares
him. The cold wind he creates is felt throughout the other circles of hell, as
well. In this section of Hell, sinners are frozen alongside Satan in a great
lake of ice.

Dante's description of the ninth circle of hell is amazingly similar to
Tolkien's description of the abyss. The tide of death that nearly froze
Gandalf's heart could easily be Dante's frozen lake.

Figure 29: Depiction of the Ninth Circle of Hell from Dante's Inferno

The Days of Gandalf's Descent and Ascent are Numbered like Christ's Descent into Hell

Tolkien takes the time to number the days of Gandalf's descent, just as Scripture numbers the days of Christ's descent. This is an important detail.

Christ descended into hell for three days between the Crucifixion and the Resurrection. Gandalf's time period was ten days. Was Christ faster because He is God? No, just kidding. I think Tolkien is doing a couple things here.

First off, there were three days between Christ's Crucifixion and Resurrection. There were ten days between Gandalf's fall from the bridge and his death. Between Gandalf's death and resurrection, he said he experienced entire "life ages" of the earth. The timeline is obviously different.

But why ten days? It is possible that Gandalf descended for three days, just like Christ, and then ascended for seven, totaling ten days in all. Seven is obviously a special number in Scripture.

While some mistakenly call it the number of perfection, the Hebrew word for seven is associated with the covenant. The Covenant between God and Creation was confected on the *seventh* day. If Gandalf died on the seventh day of his rising, Tolkien could be saying that Gandalf became a new creation on seventh day.

There is also a nod to the Sacrament of Baptism embedded in this seventh day concept, because Gandalf passes through the cold waters of death and the lake before rising, ultimately, to new life.

Both Gandalf and Christ have an Ascension

Following the descent, Gandalf ascends to the highest peak, just like the Ascension of Christ that followed His Resurrection. The order of Gandalf's ascension and resurrection is somewhat reversed from that of Christ. Nevertheless, Gandalf's physical ascension on the Endless Stair takes him to the clouds, if not the heavens.

Next, the great eagle Gwaihir actually comes and bears him up into the heavens and then on to Lothlórien, where he was clothed and replenished, and given a new staff by Galadriel. Gandalf's first ascension ends in his death and precedes the last stage of his ascension beyond death to new life.

Figure 30: The Ascension of Christ *by Rembrandt van Rijn*

Both Gandalf and Christ's Friends Fail to Recognize Them After the Resurrection

Aragorn, Legolas, and Gimli do not recognize the hooded figure of an old man that first appears to them at the edge of Fangorn Forest and scares away their horses. They actually mistake Gandalf for Saruman.

Compare this to Mary Magdalene's encounter with the risen Christ at John 20:14-15:

> She turned round and saw Jesus standing, but she did not know that it was Jesus. Jesus said to her, "Woman, why are you weeping? Whom do you seek?" **Supposing him to be the gardener**, she said to him, "Sir, if you have carried him away, tell me where you have laid him, and I will take him away."

Mary Magdalene actually confused Jesus for the gardener. She confuses him for another, just as Gandalf's friends confuse him for Saruman.

Both Gandalf and Christ are Adorned in Blinding White Clothes

Upon his resurrection, Gandalf the Gray becomes Gandalf the White. More than that, Gandalf's garments became supernaturally bright:

> There [Gandalf] stood, grown suddenly tall, towering above them. His hood and his grey rags were flung away. His white garments shone. [...] They all gazed at him. His hair was white as snow in the sunshine; and gleaming white was his robe; the eyes under his deep brows were bright, piercing as the rays of the sun; power was in his hand. Between wonder, joy, and fear they stood and found no words to say.[24]

At the Transfiguration of Christ, the Apostles are treated to an image of the Risen Christ. Matthew 17:1-2 describes the Transfiguration:

> And after six days Jesus took with him Peter and James and John his brother, and led them up a high mountain apart. And he was transfigured before them, and his face shone like the sun, and his garments became white as light.

Elsewhere, at Mark 9:3, Jesus' garments are further described as becoming "glistening, intensely white, as no fuller on earth could bleach them."

The Holy Spirit

God the Father is Eru Ilúvatar, as I've explained, but who is Tolkien's Holy Spirit? It is the Secret Fire or the Flame Imperishable, which is the power of life possessed by Eru Ilúvatar alone. Tolkien, himself, admits to this Trinitarian connection.[25]

Do you remember hearing about this Secret Fire in Lord of the Rings? It's definitely one of the best scenes from Peter Jackson's movie version. Gandalf, himself, finds his courage to stand before the Balrog of Morgoth when he calls himself a "servant of the Secret Fire":

> "You cannot pass," he said ... "I am a servant of the Secret Fire, wielder of the flame of Anor. The dark fire will not avail you, flame of Udûn. You cannot pass."[26]

I love this quote, not only because it shows how amazing Gandalf is, but also because it reveals the good and evil of Middle-Earth and the discernment needed between them. Morgoth, incidentally, is the Satan figure, a fallen member of the Valar. Sauron is merely his lieutenant.

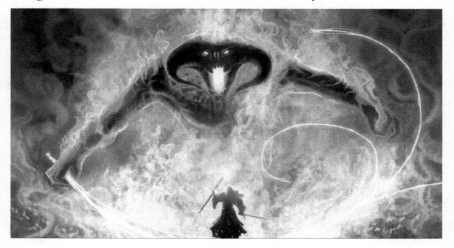

There is the Secret Fire of Eru Ilúvatar, the Holy Spirit, which is purely good and all-powerful. At war against the Secret Fire is the "dark fire." The Balrog before Gandalf was created by Tolkien's Lucifer-figure, Melkor or Morgoth, in Tolkien's Hell-equivalent, the fortress of Morgoth, Utumno or Udûn. The Balrog is the "flame of Udûn" addressed by Gandalf.

Gandalf announces that he is a servant of Tolkien's Holy Spirit before the embodiment of evil, a creature made of the dark fire, itself. Gandalf's power is rooted in his faith. He stands on that narrow bridge, the razor's edge of discernment, guided by his faith. His willingness to sacrifice himself was further rooted in his faith in the resurrection, that is, in Eru Ilúvatar, Himself. It was by the same faith that Abraham was willing to sacrifice his only son, Isaac.

The power of the dark fire can only corrupt the creations of the Secret Fire; it cannot create on its own. Isn't this a true image of evil? Of Satan? Evil can only pervert and destroy. Frodo explains this to Sam in Return of the King, as he describes the origin of orcs: "The shadow that bred them can only mock, it cannot make: not real new things of its own."[27]

God the Son: Multiple Christ Figures

There's no single Christ, Messiah, or God-the-Son in Tolkien's mythology – this could be the subject of further discussions, i.e. The Christs of Lord of the Rings. God the Son, as a person of the Trinity, is splintered among many different characters. Ultimately, all the heroes of literature, insofar as they are heroes or anti-heroes, are images of Christ. In Tolkien, the other persons of the Trinity, God the Father and God the Holy Spirit, are not splintered and are somewhat straightforward.

As I said, there's more than one Christ figure in *The Lord of the Rings*. Tolkien splintered his Messiah into at least three characters: Gandalf, Frodo, and, of course, Aragorn. Each of these characters represents a different aspect of Christ:

- Gandalf the Grey (and White) represents the Resurrection, but more importantly he represents the third person of the Trinity, The Word, who exists outside of time.

- Frodo Baggins represents the Sacrifice (the Crucifixion), the journey which begins in sleepy, out-of-the-way Nazareth and ends on the slopes of Golgotha.

- Aragorn, son of Arathorn represents the King, the restoration of the Davidic Kingdom.

Is Tolkien's Trinity a true Trinity?

Eru Ilúvatar never exists, truly, in three persons. Though Tolkien has Christ figures, his Trinity does not include a full-fledged God, the Son, much less is Ilúvatar actually incarnated.

Further, the Flame Imperishable does not seem to exist as a person or as equal to Ilúvatar. Rather, the Secret Fire seems to be something that is possessed by Ilúvatar.

An Old Testament Trinity

Tolkien's Trinity is not a New Testament Trinity. It more closely resembles the Trinity as expressed in the Old Testament. In the Old Testament, the Trinity is only partially revealed. Also, Tolkien's Trinity is most developed in its act of creation.

Compare Tolkien's creation to the Book of Genesis. In Genesis, God the Son is the Word spoken at creation. He appears in Scripture whenever Wisdom and Truth are spoken of in capital letters. God the Holy Spirit is present at creation, also, as the spirit moving over the waters (Gen 1:2). This very similar to *The Lord of the Rings*:

- The Son: the first of the creations of Eru Ilúvatar, the Ainu, were born of his thought, much as God spoke the Word at creation.

- The Holy Spirit: The Flame Imperishable is the power of life possessed by Eru Ilúvatar alone, similar to the Spirit of God which is active in creation across the formlessness.

The doctrine of the Trinity will not be fully revealed until the Gospels and Paul's epistles. Even then, it will take several hundred years of Church history and not a few heresies to arrive at something approaching a full explanation. This is how doctrine develops: as "through a mirror dimly" which clears through the passage of time (1 Cor 13:12).

St. Augustine was warned by an angel not to expect too much of his feeble mind when investigating the mysteries of the Trinity. Tolkien seems to heed the same warning; the creation of Middle-Earth is not simply a recapitulation of the Genesis story. His imagination has great power. Tolkien reveals the infinite wonder which can be found in just the natures of God and creation.

Aragorn as Christ: The Return of the King

Much of this section has already been described in the first section of this book. Aragorn is Isildur's heir, who restores the kingdom of men. Christ is the "son of [King] David" and "the branch" who will restore the Kingdom of David. This section runs deep!

There are some additional Christ-like characteristics to Aragorn:

- The king in *Lord of the Rings* is prophesied to have the hands of a healer. Likewise, Christ goes about healing the sick, lepers, etc.

- The Númenóreans, the Race of Kings, are gifted with extraordinarily long lifespans. Likewise, the Bible describes the long lives of the early Patriarchs, such as Adam and Methuselah

- The statue of Aragorn's mother in Rivendell looks very familiar. It could even be mistaken for a statue of the Blessed Mother.

Endnotes:

[21] Carpenter, Humphrey, ed. (1981), The Letters of J. R. R. Tolkien, Boston: Houghton Mifflin, #153, ISBN 0-395-31555-7.

[22] Fellowship of the Ring

[23] *The Two Towers*, "The White Rider"

[24] *The Two Towers*, LOTR Book III, Ch. 5, "The White Rider".

[25] Clyde S. Kilby. *Tolkien & The Silmarillion*. Harold Shaw, 1976, p. 59.

[26] *The Fellowship of the Ring,* LOTR Book II, Ch. 5, "The Bridge of Khazad-dûm".

[27] Tolkien, J. R. R., The Return of the King VI 1: "The Tower of Cirith Ungol"

THE THEOLOGY OF THE ENTS

W here did all these armies of trees – Tolkien's Ents and Huorns, Shakespeare's Birnam Wood, even Kurosawa's *Throne of Blood* – come from? The Bible, of course.

In *The Lord of the Rings: The Two Towers*, the Ents march on Saruman's fortress of Orthanc in Isengard and are an unstoppable force and just plain awesome. Also, the Huorns, who are either Ents who have turned treeish or trees that have grown wild and grumpy, march from Fangorn forest. In the movie version, they consume the retreating Uruk-hai from the Battle of the Hornburg at Helm's Deep.

Ents Versus Huorns

The trees of the Great Forests came from the seeds that Yavanna created in the Age of the Lamps. They are among the most ancient of the Olvar.

In the Ages of the Stars, great spirits came among the trees as their protectors. These protector spirits became known as Ents.

As ages passed, it is said that the Ents became more treeish and the ancient trees became more Ent-like, learning the art of speech. By the Third Age, these Ent-like trees had become a race apart, the Huorns.

According to the *Tolkien Encyclopaedia*, the Huorns mostly stood as dark trees in the deepest forests, gnarled and unmoving, yet watchful. When aroused in wrath they moved swiftly as if wrapped in shadows, falling on foes with deadly and merciless strength.[28]

In the War of the Ring, the Ents and the Huorns, "like a great forest," marched on Isengard and then exterminated the entire Orc legion in the Battle of the Hornburg at Helm's Deep.

What was Old Man Willow?

Incidentally, the hobbits encounter huorns elsewhere besides Fangorn forest. Frodo and the others encountered a huorn in the Old Forest, as well. They found him along the banks of the Withywindle River. This was Old Man Willow.

The Old Forest and Fangorn were the last remnants of the ancient forests of Middle-Earth. Old Man Willow had grown angry over the slow destruction of his forest.

By the time the hobbits wandered near, the power of his song enchanted their entire wood leading all travelers to him and his encircling roots and branches. The hobbits almost met their end buried beneath Old Man Willow, but for the intercession of Tom Bombadil.

Figure 31: Old Man Willow, illustration by the Brothers Hildebrandt

What was Tolkien's inspiration for the Ents?

In a letter to the Anglo-American poet, W. H. Auden, Tolkien explains his inspiration for the Ents:

> Their part in the story is due, I think, to my bitter disappointment and disgust from schooldays with the shabby use made in Shakespeare of the coming of "Great Birnam wood to high Dunsinane hill": I longed to devise a setting in which the trees might really march to war. And into this has crept a mere piece of experience, the difference of the "male" and "female" attitude to wild things, the difference between unpossessive love and gardening.[29]

Tolkien's Ents and Huorns were inspired by the marching of Shakespeare's Birnam Wood at the end of MacBeth.

Do you remember that part of the play? At Act 4, Scene 1, the Third Apparition appears in the form of a child with a crown on his head and a *tree* in his hand. The ghost child says the following before descending:

> Be brave like the lion and proud. Don't even worry about who hates you, who resents you, and who conspires against you. Macbeth will never be defeated until Birnam Wood marches to fight you at Dunsinane Hill.

In Scene 3, MacBeth tells that doctor that he is not afraid of an invasion because of the three witches' prediction that (1) No man born of woman can kill him and (2) the woods must march before he is defeated. Well, guess what? Both of these things happen.

The First Prophecy

On a side note, do you remember how Tolkien also used the first of the witches' prophecies, that "no man born of woman can kill him"? Sound familiar? The elf Glorfindel made a similar prophesy about The Witch-King of Angmar, "Do not pursue him! He will not return to these lands. Far off yet is his doom, and not by the hand of man will he fall."[30]

Figure 32: Movie stills from Return of the King, *Copyright New Line Cinema*

The Witch-King's doom comes at the hands of Eowyn. Just before smiting the leader of the Nazgûl, Eowyn fulfills Glorfindel's prophesy with the words, "I am no man!" She slays the Witch-King with help of Merry, who, again, is not a man but a hobbit.

For Shakespeare, this prophesy was likely inspired by the Proto-Evangelium ("First Gospel") of Genesis 3:15:

I will put enmity between you and the woman,
and between your seed and her seed;
He shall bruise your head, and
you shall bruise his heel.

The "seed" of woman can only refer to one man in all of human history. One man! Elsewhere in the Bible or other ancient documents you will only ever see the "seed of man," not woman. There is only one man in human history who had no earthly father, who was born of a virgin. This is, of course, Jesus of Nazareth born of the Virgin Mary and conceived by the Holy Spirit.

That's kind of shocking, isn't it? The whole Gospel was contained in one verse of Genesis. The whole of salvation history was outlined from the beginning. God wasn't making it up as He went. The most ancient prophesy of the Messiah is surprisingly clear:

a virgin birth who will strike at the skull of the serpent. Where was Christ crucified? Into what place was the wood of Christ's cross thrust? What was the place's name? Golgotha, which means "place of the skull." Incredible!

What's more, there is a legend that Golgotha received its name as the burial place of Adam. This is why a skull is typically depicted at the foot of the cross in classic artwork. But that's the subject of other writings.

The Second Prophecy

Back to *MacBeth*. In Scene 4, Malcolm instructs his army, "let every soldier hew him down a bough." The soldiers cover themselves in the branches of Birnam Wood and advance upon Dunsinane Castle, fulfilling the prophesy:

> As I did stand my watch upon the hill, I look'd toward Birnam, and anon, methought, The wood began to move. (Messenger, Scene V)

Figure 33: This picture shows Malcolm's soldiers carrying the branches of Birnam Wood toward Dunsinane Castle

But what was Shakespeare's inspiration?

The books of the Prophet Samuel detail, in part, the wars, rebellions, and conquests of King David. When Absalom rebels against his father David, David retreats to Ephraim Wood. Absalom pursues David into the wood, and his armies are completely destroyed. But David had some help:

> So the army went out into the field against Israel; and the battle was fought in **the forest of E′phraim.** And the men of Israel were defeated there by the servants of David, and the slaughter there was great on that day, twenty thousand men. The battle spread out over that entire region, and **the thickets consumed more combatants that day than did the sword.** (2 Samuel 18:8)

Absalom, himself, was snatched from his mule by the branches of an oak tree and struggled there until Joab thrust three spears into him.

Absalom is also a type for Christ. Absalom's death by hanging from a tree foreshadows Christ's death hanging from a tree, i.e. the Cross. Note, also, that three wounds marked the Sacred Heart of Jesus, the Son of the King, as he hung from the wood of the cross. Of course, Christ, unlike Absalom, was blameless.

Figure 34: The Death of Absalom, Schnorr von Carolsfeld, Julius 1794– 1874.

This description of the Battle of Ephraim Wood directly inspired Shakespeare's *MacBeth*, and in so doing inspired Tolkien. It's also entirely possible the Tolkien was directly inspired by Scripture, too.

MacBeth has other parallels to struggles between King David and Absalom. For example, the announcement to MacDuff of his family's death is very similar to the announcement to David of Absalom's death.[31]

More interesting still, Shakespeare was also bereaved from the loss of his own son, Hamnet – of course, this same wellspring of pain and suffering gave birth to another Shakespearean tragedy: *Hamlet*.

Endnotes:

[28] Day, David. *Tolkien: The Illustrated Encyclopaedia*. Simon & Schuster, 1991: 206.

[29] Humphrey Carpenter, *The Letters of J.R.R. Tolkien* (New York, NY: Houghton Mifflin, 2000), Letter #163.

[30] *The Return of the King*, Appendix A (I, iv)

[31] E. Littel, "Letters to the Young," The Religious Magazine; Or, Spirit of the Foreign Theological Journals and Reviews, Vol. II, 1828, p. 376.

NOTES ON TOLKIEN'S VIRGIN MARY

A ll these chapters about the Trinity, Christ figures, and the Eucharist, you would think I would cover Tolkien's representations of the Blessed Mother, too, right? That might be a whole, other book. J.R.R. Tolkien said the following about the Virgin Mary:

> I think I know exactly what you mean by the order of Grace; and, of course, by your references to Our Lady, upon which all my own small perception of beauty both in majesty and simplicity is founded.[32]

All of Tolkien's perception of beauty is founded on the Blessed Mother, and there is quite a lot of beauty in the Tolkien's writing.

Just as there are three Christ figures in *The Lord of the Rings*, there are also three Marian figures, a Trinity of each.

The three Christs are each linked to one of three Marys:

Frodo to Eowyn: They are both wounded by the sword of a Nazgul. This is similar to Simeon's prophesy about Christ and His Mother at the Presentation of Jesus in the Temple. Simeon prophesizes at Luke 2:35 that "a sword shall pierce your heart, as well", referring to Mary's future suffering.

Aragorn to Arwen: Arwen is the immortal bride of the King. Similarly, the Church, which Mary represents, is the spotless bride of Christ, which will last forever and the "gates of hell will not prevail against [her]" (Matthew 16:18).

Gandalf to Galadriel: Both ancient figures. Peter Jackson's version of The Hobbit even hints at a certain amount of affection between the two. Galadriel is significant for several other reasons, as well, as described below.

Galadriel

There are several Marian aspects to Galadriel. First off, as we have already discussed, Galadriel is significant for the giving of gifts, including the Lembas Bread and daggers for the journey of the Fellowship. The Lembas Bread has been rigorously examined as the Eucharist above.

Galadriel is also a Queen Mother. She is the grandmother of Arwen. This is not a direct connection because Galadriel's husband, Celeborn, rules as king, not her son as is the case with the Kingdom of Israel.

The Queen Mother is a significant feature of the Kingdom of Israel. This is the royal office of the *Gebirah*. The Queen-Mother sat in a throne beside the King of Israel, such as King Solomon as described in 1 Kings 2. The Queen-Mother received petitions ("prayers") from the people of Israel and interceded before the king.

Gimli, for example, petitions Galadriel for strands of her hair. Galadriel also gives the Light of Eärendil's star, the light of the Two Trees as preserved in a Silmaril. The Two Trees are also a significant reference to the two trees of Eden, the Tree of Life and the Tree of Knowledge of Good & Evil.

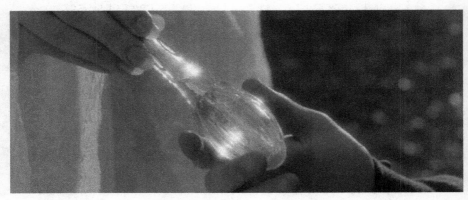

Figure 35: Movie still from The Fellowship of the Ring, *Galadriel giving Frodo the Light of Earendil, Copyright New Line Cinema*

Galadriel was also born was born in Valinor during the Years of the Trees before the First Age had even begun. This is interesting because Galadriel is a figure of both Eve and the New Eve, Mary.

Like Eve, Galadriel was exiled to Middle-Earth. She was not permitted to make the journey to the Undying Lands.[33] So, why do we see Galadriel leaving for the Undying Lands along with Gandalf and Celeborn at the end of *The Lord of the Rings*?

Galadriel's ban was lifted because she refused the One Ring.[34] Galadriel overcame the temptation to take the Ring from Frodo.

The sin of Eve is unwound by the obedience of the New Eve, Mary. Eve, like Galadriel, is exiled for sin. The New Eve, Mary, releases all people from their exile through her obedience.

St. Irenaeus of Lyons describes this succinctly: "The knot of Eve's disobedience was loosed by the obedience of Mary. For what the virgin Eve had bound fast through unbelief, this did the Virgin Mary set free through faith."

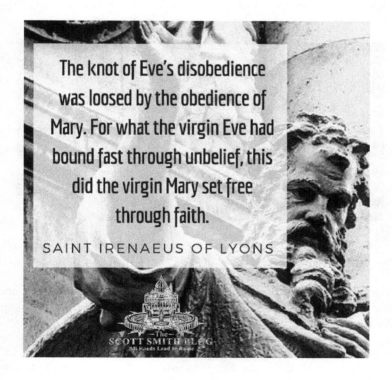

The knot of Eve's disobedience was loosed by the obedience of Mary. For what the virgin Eve had bound fast through unbelief, this did the virgin Mary set free through faith.

SAINT IRENAEUS OF LYONS

—The—
SCOTT SMITH BLOG
All Roads Lead to Rome

Eowyn

As described above, Eowyn's fulfills the prophecy of the Witch-King who will not be killed by any man "born of woman". This is similar to the prophecy in *MacBeth*, which is itself similar to the "seed of woman" prophecy in Genesis 3:15, the Protoevangelium.

Also, as discussed in this chapter already, Eowyn is connected to Frodo in that they are both wounded by the Nazgul, wounds "which will never fully heal" or, as in Luke 2:35, "a sword shall also pierce your heart"

Aragorn's Mother

Aragorn is one of the most significant and obvious Christ figures in *The Lord of the Rings*. Therefore, we ought to examine the descriptions of his mother for Marian features.

At least in the movie version of *The Lord of the Rings*, Aragorn's mother is Marian in appearance. The statue of Gilraen, Aragorn's mother, strongly resembles a statue of Mary with her mantle, etc. See below:

Gilraen's name means "Wandering Star". Similarly, several of Mary's titles are related to stars, such as "Star of the Sea" and "Morning Star".

Gilraen's father, Dírhael, was opposed to Gilraen's marriage to Aragorn's father because he felt Gilraen was too young to marry and because he had a sense of foreboding that Arathorn would not live long. Likewise, Mary was engaged to marry Joseph at a very young age.

After Aragorn's husband is slain by an orc arrow, Gilraen seeks shelter for her son in Rivendell under the protection of Elrond. This is similar to Mary and Joseph's flight into Egypt to protect the Christ child following Herod's slaughter of the innocents.

Figure 36: Statue of Gilraen in Rivendell

Endnotes:

[32] *The Philosophy of Tolkien: The Worldview Behind The Lord of the Rings*, p. 76.
[33] In "The Road Goes Ever On" it is stated that "at the end of the First Age, a ban was set on her return, and she had replied proudly that she had no wish to do so."
[34] From Tolkien's Letters # 297

Bonus Section:
THE CATHOLIC
THEOLOGY OF
STAR WARS

The Virgin Birth of Star Wars

I'm pretty sure I saw *Star Wars* in the womb. I'm pretty sure that the first time I heard the trumpet blast of the score of *A New Hope*, I was encased in amniotic fluid. I was actually born the day after *Return of the Jedi* was released.

It is such sweet satisfaction to know that the origins of Star Wars, too, were Catholic.

We should probably expect this from a series of movies in which the heroes are running around in cassocks like a Franciscan. The robes of the Jedi are obviously the robes of Catholic monks. Instead of rosaries handing from their belts, the Jedi have lightsabers. I would argue that the rosary is, at the very least, as powerful as a lightsaber. More powerful, even, take the Battle of Lepanto, for example. The Rosary conquered a whole army.

The Jedi speak of an ancient prophesy that is fulfilled by the birth and life of Anakin Skywalker. Clearly, the subject of the prophecy is a Messiah figure. This is made blatantly obvious when we discover that he is the seed of woman (Gen 3:15) alone, that he was **conceived by the Force,** that Shmi gave birth as a virgin.

Hello, McFly! This is one of the most obvious connections in all the galaxies in all the universes of science fiction.

The Prophesy of the Chosen One

"You refer to the prophecy of the one who will bring balance to the Force. You believe it's this...boy?"

—Mace Windu

The Prophesy of the Chosen One spoke of the coming of a savior who would bring balance to the Force. It was also referred to as the Prophecy of the Son of the Suns. The Chosen One was also referred to as the Son of Suns. Sound familiar? The King of Kings? Also, speaking of "suns", remember the iconic image of Luke contemplating his destiny before the setting Twin Suns of Tatooine?

And then the blare of the lone trumpet as the "Force Theme" is played during the binary sunset ...

And the same shot again with baby Luke in the arms of Uncle Owen and Aunt Beru ...

Ophuchi Clan & the Desert

The only known keepers of information regarding the prophecy, besides the Jedi, were the Ophuchi Clan. The Ophuchi were a monastic sect of hermits living an aesthetic life in the Dune Sea of Tatooine.

According to the *Journal of the Whills*, the most ancient and complete record of galactic history, "For it is written, the Ophuchi shall inherit the desert." The obvious reference here is to the Beatitudes: "blessed are the meek, for they shall inherit the earth" (Matthew 5:5).

Figure 14: Icon of the Prophet Elijah

The Ophuchi were actually founded by Elias in 12,977 BBY. Elias, of course, is a name shared by one of the greatest prophets in Scripture: Elijah. In Hebrew, this name means "My God is Jehovah."

Wouldn't it be interesting if – despite the "a long time ago in a Galaxy far, far away" business – if Star Wars was a depiction of mankind's distant future, a future which is still being shaped by the prophets of Yahweh and still governed by the Jehovah? Islam, too, hails Elijah as a great prophet, a "prophet of the desert—like John the Baptist."[35] The association of the desert, Tatooine, Elijah, and the Ophuchi is, of course, no coincidence.

The Jedi Version

The Jedi version of the Prophesy was written down and ascribed to ancient Jedi philosophers. The Jedi prophesy described the birth of One who would destroy the Sith and bring the force back into balance. The imbalance in the Force was due to the misuse of the Force by the dark side.

Both Obi-Wan Kenobi and Qui-Gon Jinn believed that Anakin Skywalker was the Chosen One, and that he would bring about the final destruction of the Sith. Yoda cautioned against a hasty interpretation, giving the following warning: "A prophecy that misread might have been."

Some would argue that Luke, not Anakin, was the Chosen One, but none other than George Lucas, himself, later confirmed that the Chosen One was Anakin. Why is that? Because only Anakin was born of a virgin.

Who was the Virgin Mother?

All this talk of a Virgin birth. Well, who was the Virgin Mother? Shmi Skywalker Lars:

Let's stop for a second to consider how important this woman is to Star Wars galaxy. She is the mother and only human parent of Anakin Skywalker, Darth Vader. She is the original owner of C-3PO. She is the grandmother to both Luke Skywalker and Princess Leia Organa. She is the mother-in-law to Han Solo. She is also the great-grandmother to Ben Solo, who would become Kylo Ren. One big, happy family, right?

If Shmi – or should we say Granny Skywalker? – gave birth despite being a virgin, how was Anakin conceived? The explanation we are given is that Anakin was conceived miraculously by the Force, itself, through the working of the midichlorians.

So, wait a second, an unseen, invisible *force* conceives a child within the virgin? This is the second part of the Scriptural parallel. ***The Force is the Holy Spirit.***

Let's compare this to the Gospel of Luke. That's Luke the Evangelist, by the way, not Skywalker. So many connections!

> And Mary said to the angel, "How can this be, since I have no husband?" And the angel said to her,

> "The Holy Spirit will come upon you, and the power of the Most High will overshadow you; therefore the child to be born will be called holy, the Son of God ..." (Luke 1: 34-35)

The child who is born of the Virgin will be called holy, the Son of God, and "the Lord will give to him the throne of his father."

The prophesy of the Messiah is nearly identical to the prophesy of the Chosen One. Darth Vader will even later offer Luke his throne, so they can "rule the Galaxy as father and son."

The Tragedy of Darth Plagueis "the Wise"

There's much more, though. Did you notice the conversation between Senator Palpatine and Anakin in the *Revenge of the Sith*? Palpatine was telling Anakin of his own Sith master, Darth Plagueis.

Think about how twisted this is. Palpatine was actually telling Anakin the origin of the prophesy about HIS OWN BIRTH.

Figure 15: Movie still, Senator Palpatine speaking to Anakin

Here is how Senator Palpatine tells the story, according to the movie:

> Did you ever hear the tragedy of Darth Plagueis "the wise"? I thought not. It's not a story the Jedi would tell you. It's a Sith legend.
>
> Darth Plagueis was a Dark Lord of the Sith, so powerful and so wise he could use the Force to influence the midichlorians to create life... He had such a knowledge of the dark side that he could even keep the ones he cared about from dying.
>
> The dark side of the Force is a pathway to many abilities some consider to be unnatural.
>
> He became so powerful... the only thing he was afraid of was losing his power, which eventually, of course, he did.
>
> Unfortunately, he taught his apprentice everything he knew, then his apprentice killed him in his sleep. It's ironic he could save others from death, but not himself.

This Darth Plagueis twist is fantastic storytelling. Listen to this. The story continues beyond what Senator Palpatine reveals. Palpatine is incredibly devious. He ends the story prematurely, before he would reveal to Anakin the mystery of his own birth.

This is the rest of the story: Darth Plagueis, Emperor Palpatine's Sith master, whom he killed, never actually died. Instead, Plagueis *ascended* into the Force. He subsumed himself into it, using his own power over life and death.

Darth Plagueis had not only learned how to keep people from dying, but how to prevent *himself* from dying. Doesn't this all sound like a dark, twisted version of the Resurrection and the Ascension of Jesus?

There's more! Darth Plagueis raised himself into the Force, so that he could be born again, re-conceived by the Force, itself, and become more powerful than ever before. Plagueis succeeded with the virgin birth of Anakin Skywalker.

But think about it – Plagueis did more than this. He achieved his revenge against Palpatine through Anakin! *Who eventually kills the man who killed Plagueis?* Anakin does, or rather Darth Vader does. The circle of revenge is completed when Vader kills Emperor Palpatine.

Isn't it ironic--and proof of the Palpatine's terrible cunning rhetoric and half-truths --that Anakin was finally taken over to the Dark Side by his belief that Palpatine could teach Anakin to save Padmé's life? Stupid Anakin, you're the one who taught Palpatine in your previous Incarnation as Plagueis!

I doubt that the Star Wars prophesy goes so far as to support the doctrine of the Immaculate Conception, which is too bad, but you have to ask the question: why and how did Darth Plagueis pick and prepare Shmi, on sandy, desolate, nowhere Tatooine (read "Nazareth"), to be his mother?

George Lucas, Joseph Campbell, & Myths

Obviously, this is not a pure retelling of the Virgin Birth. For one, it's a contrived, maybe even forced, pregnancy by an evil Sith Lord.

Also, there seems to be a bit of Hinduism and Buddhism in this imaginative restructuring of the Virgin Birth. The birth of Anakin seems more like a RE-incarnation, than an Incarnation.

George Lucas amalgamated, lumped together, and synthesized several different hero stories to create the Star Wars galaxy. It would better if Lucas didn't muddy up the Gospel. I can hardly blame him, though, for using elements of the greatest events in human history to structure his stories.

Lucas was a big fan of Joseph Campbell. Campbell created the idea of the monomyth. This is the idea, basically, that all of mankind's hero stories are one. The hero's journey is remarkably similar across every world culture.

Why is this? Joseph Campbell would say, following the ideas of Carl Jung, that the hero archetype is built into human nature. That's why the same stories appear again and again, from Hercules to Spiderman, throughout human history.

I would say there's a bigger reason for this. The Hero of Heroes, the King of Kings, Jesus Christ, exists outside of time. God has been preparing us throughout time for His Son. God prepared man through his dreams. His imagination.

Every myth that preceded Jesus' life was a dream of our coming Savior. We understood, subconsciously or through a collective unconscious, who he would be. Jesus' life was of such magnitude as to ripple through history, forward and backward.

Not only that, we were told! God told us "in the beginning". The Messiah was described to our first parents in Genesis 3:15, the Proto-Evangelium.

The Heresy of Darth Plagueis

One last thing ... there is an ancient Christian heresy which was begun by Pelagius (doesn't that name sound familiar?). Isn't the resemblance funny? Plagueis looks like he is wearing Sith robes:

None less than Saint Augustine fought the Pelagian heresy. The heresy held that man, by his own power, could perfect himself. Man, without the grace of God, could make himself sinless. Taking the power of life and death, of sin and death, into one's own hands sounds remarkably like what Darth Plagueis taught.

Endnotes:

[32] *The Philosophy of Tolkien: The Worldview Behind The Lord of the Rings*, p. 76.

[33] In "The Road Goes Ever On" it is stated that "at the end of the First Age, a ban was set on her return, and she had replied proudly that she had no wish to do so."

[34] From Tolkien's Letters # 297

[35] Abdullah Yusuf Ali, *The Holy Qur'an: Text, Translation and Commentary*, Note. 4112.

HOLYWATERBOOKS

About the Author:
Scott L. Smith, Jr.

Scott L. Smith, Jr. is a Catholic author, attorney, and theologian. He and his wife Ashton are the parents of five wild-eyed children and live in their hometown of New Roads, Louisiana.

Smith is currently serving as the Chairman of the Men of the Immaculata, the Grand Knight of his local Knights of Columbus council, and a co-host of the Catholic Nerds Podcast. Smith has served as a minister and teacher far and wide: from Angola, Louisiana's maximum-security prison, to the slums of Kibera, Kenya.

Smith's books include _Pray the Rosary with St. Pope John Paul II_, _The Catholic ManBook_, _Everything You Need to Know About Mary But Were Never Taught_, _The Theology of Sci-Fi: The Christian's Companion to the Galaxy_, and _Blessed is He Who ... (Biographies of Blesseds)_. Smith is also the author of the first pro-life horror novel, _The Seventh Word_.

Scott regularly contributes to his blog, "The Scott Smith Blog" at www.thescottsmithblog.com, WINNER of the Fisher's Net Award for Best Catholic Blog:

FISHER'S NET AWARD
BEST CATHOLIC
BLOG 2018

— THE —
SCOTT SMITH BLOG
ALL ROADS LEAD TO ROME

AS SEEN ON ...
NATIONAL CATHOLIC
REGISTER
ChurchPOP
Aleteia
BIG PULPIT
New Advent
Catholic Online
SPIRIT DAILY
ALL
SAINTS
UNIVERSITY
CATHOLICISM.ORG

Scott's other books can be found at his publisher's, Holy Water Books, website, holywaterbooks.com, as well as on Amazon.

His other books on theology and the Catholic faith include _Lord of the Rings & the Eucharist_, _The Catholic ManBook_, _Everything You Need to Know About Mary But Were Never Taught_, _The Theology of Sci-Fi: The Christian's Companion to the Galaxy_, and _Blessed is He Who ... (Biographies of Blesseds)_. More on these below ...

His fiction includes _The Seventh Word_, a pro-life horror novel, and the _Cajun Zombie Chronicles_, the Catholic version of the zombie apocalypse.

More Classic Catholic Reprints!

THE SPIRITUAL COMBAT:
THE CLASSIC MANUAL ON SPIRITUAL WARFARE
BY DOM LORENZO SCUPOLI

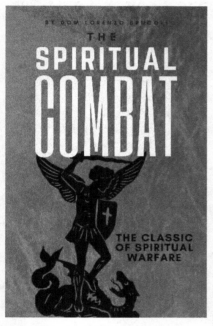

St. Francis de Sales always carried this book in his pocket!

The Spiritual Combat is the classic manual of spiritual warfare. Its wisdom has helped form the souls of the Church's greatest saints. Now this book can do the same thing for you.

It's no longer fashionable to speak about the realities of the devil and demons, and so the world has become more vulnerable than ever before. The Christian life is a battle between God and the forces of darkness.

This is the Art of War for the Christian. Pick up your sword and fight! Here, Father Lorenzo Scupoli helps guide you through this spiritual battle, so that you can win - decisively - the war for your soul.

This is the classic work on spiritual combat. Loved by saints and sinners alike ever since it was first written four hundred years ago. Why? It provides straight-forward, practical, sensible advice to help you daily overcome the devil's temptations and other spiritual obstacles to achieve spiritual perfection.

This battle-ready advice includes:
- 12 ways to contemplate death to help you live better now
- 7 reflections to help you be sorry for sinning

- 7 powerful methods of prayer
- Pushing through dry periods, when prayer is difficult and burdensome

Pick up the sword of prayer and conquer the evil which afflicts you, and through you, your family, your friends, and the world. Don't go into battle alone. Go with Christ and this classic combat manual.

THE SEVEN LAST WORDS SPOKEN FROM THE CROSS
by St. Robert Bellarmine S.J.

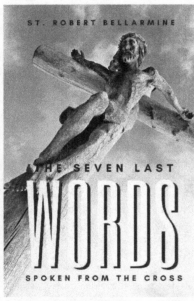

Come, sit at the foot of the Cross!

These seven words were the "last sermon" of the Savior of the World. Jesus' words from the Cross contain everything that the prophets foretold about His preaching, suffering, and miracles.

The Seven Last Words Spoken from the Cross is a powerful reflection on the final words of Jesus Christ. The author, St. Robert Bellarmine, was a major figure in the Catholic Counter-Reformation and his insights are as profound now as ever, perhaps more than ever.

Deepen the Way of the Cross! Use Bellarmine's contemplations of Christ's words to enrich your Lenten journey to Good Friday and Easter. The Seven Last Words Spoken from the Cross is a wealth of insights for the whole of the Christian life, which points always to Christ, who was lifted up on the Cross so "that everyone who believes in Him may have eternal life."

Pray, Hope, & Don't Worry:
Catholic Prayer Journal for Women

Scott also recently authored a series of prayer journals with his wife. *The Pray, Hope, & Don't Worry* Prayer Journal to Overcome Stress and Anxiety:

ALL
SAINTS
UNIVERSITY
EST. MMXVII

Scott has also produced courses on the Blessed Mother and Scripture for All Saints University.

Learn about the Blessed Mary from anywhere and learn to defend your mother! It includes over six hours of video plus a free copy of the next book … Enroll Now!

What You *Need* to Know About Mary
But Were Never Taught

St. Louis de Montfort's Total Consecration to Jesus through Mary: New, Day-by-Day, Easier-to-Read Translation

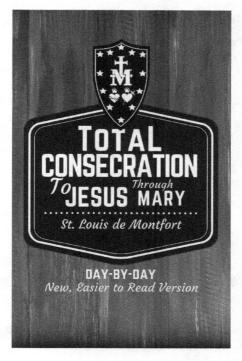

Popes and Saints have called this single greatest book of Marian spirituality ever written. In a newly translated day-by-day format, follow St. Louis de Montfort's classic work on the spiritual way to Jesus Christ though the Blessed Virgin Mary. Beloved by countless souls, this book sums up, not just the majesty of the Blessed Mother, but the entire Christian life. St. Louis de Montfort calls this the "short, easy, secure, and perfect" path to Christ. It is the way chosen by Jesus, Himself.

Pray the Rosary with St. John Paul II

St. John Paul II said "the Rosary is my favorite prayer." So what could possibly make praying the Rosary even better? Praying the Rosary with St. John Paul II!

This book includes a reflection from John Paul II for every mystery of the Rosary. You will find John Paul II's biblical reflections on the twenty mysteries of the Rosary that provide practical insights to help

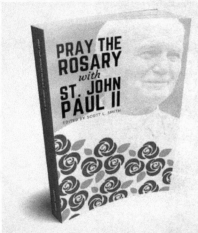

you not only understand the twenty mysteries but also live them.

St. John Paul II said "The Rosary is my favorite prayer. A marvelous prayer! Marvelous in its simplicity and its depth. In the prayer we repeat many times the words that the Virgin Mary heard from the Archangel, and from her kinswoman Elizabeth."

St. John Paul II said "the Rosary is the storehouse of countless blessings." In this new book, he will help you dig even deeper into the treasures contained within the Rosary.

You will also learn St. John Paul II's spirituality of the Rosary: "To pray the Rosary is to hand over our burdens to the merciful hearts of Christ and His mother."

"The Rosary, though clearly Marian in character, is at heart a Christ-centered prayer. It has all the depth of the gospel message in its entirety. It is an echo of the prayer of Mary, her perennial Magnificat for the work of the redemptive Incarnation which began in her virginal womb."

Take the Rosary to a whole new level with St. John Paul the Great! St. John Paul II, *pray for us!*

Prayer Like a Warrior:
Spiritual Combat & War Room Prayer Guide

Don't get caught unarmed! Develop your Prayer Room Strategy and Battle Plan.

An invisible war rages around you. Something or someone is attacking you, unseen, unheard, yet felt throughout every aspect of your life. An army of demons under the banner of Satan has a singular focus: your destruction and that of everyone you know and love.

You need to protect your soul, your heart, your mind, your marriage, your children, your relationships, your resolve, your dreams, and your destiny.

Do you want to be a Prayer Warrior, but don't know where to start? The Devil's battle plan depends on catching you unarmed and unaware. If you're tired of being pushed around and wrecked by sin and distraction, this book is for you.

Do you feel uncomfortable speaking to God? Do you struggle with distractions in the presence of Almighty God? Praying to God may feel foreign, tedious, or like a ritual, and is He really listening? What if He never hears, never responds? This book will show you that God always listens and always answers.

In this book, you will learn how to prayer effectively no matter where you are mentally, what your needs are, or how you are feeling:

- Prayers when angry or your heart is troubled
- Prayers for fear, stress, and hopelessness
- Prayers to overcome pride, unforgiveness, and bitterness
- Prayers for rescue and shelter

Or are you looking to upgrade your prayer life? This book is for you, too. You already know that a prayer war room is a powerful weapon in spiritual warfare. Prepare for God to pour out blessings on your life.

Author, theologian, and attorney Scott L. Smith, Jr. has tested the prayers and wisdom of this book as a missionary in Africa, a minister in maximum security prisons, in the courtroom, and, most challenging of all, as a husband and father of four.

Our broken world and broken souls need the prayers and direction found in this book. Don't waste time fumbling through your prayer life. Pray more strategically when you have a War Room Battle Plan. Jesus showed His disciples how to pray and He wants to show you how to pray, too.

Catholic Nerds Podcast

As you might have noticed, Scott is obviously well-credentialed as a nerd. Check out Scott's podcast: the Catholic Nerds Podcast on iTunes, Podbean, Google Play, and wherever good podcasts are found!

The Theology of Sci-Fi:
The Christian's Companion to the Galaxy

Fold space using the spice mélange and travel from "a long time ago in a galaxy far, far away" to the planet Krypton, from Trantor to Terminus, and back to the scorched skies of earth.

Did you know there is a Virgin Birth at the core of *Star Wars*? A Jewish Messiah of *Dune*? A Holy Family in *Superman*? A Jesus and Judas in *The Matrix*? And the Catholic Church is Asimov's *Foundation*?

This book covers a lot of territory. It spans galaxies and universes. Nevertheless, the great expanse of human imagination will forever be captivated by the events of the little town of Bethlehem.

There is a reason that all of mankind's stories overlap, coincide, correlate, and copy. Like it or not, all mankind bears the same indelible stamp, the mark of Christ. Why should there be a singular story binding us all? Unless we are truly all bound as one human family. At the core of the Monomyth is not another myth, a neat coincidence, but a reality—the reality of Jesus Christ.

At the heart of the Monomyth is a man, a very real man. The God-Man. The source and summit of all hero stories and myths ever told, both before and after those short 33 years in First Century Israel.

What You Need to Know About Mary But Were Never Taught

Give a robust defense of the Blessed Mother using Scripture. Now, more than ever, every Catholic needs to learn how to defend their mother, the Blessed Mother. Because now, more than ever, the family is under attack and needs its Mother.

Discover the love story, hidden within the whole of Scripture, of the Father for his daughter, the Holy Spirit for his spouse, and the Son for his MOTHER.

This collection of essays and the All Saints University course made to accompany it will demonstrate through Scripture how the Immaculate Conception of Mary was prophesied in Genesis.

It will also show how the Virgin Mary is the New Eve, the New Ark, and the New Queen of Israel.

The Catholic ManBook

Do you want to reach Catholic Man LEVEL: EXPERT? *The Catholic ManBook* is your handbook to achieving Sainthood, manly Sainthood. Find the following resources inside, plus many others:

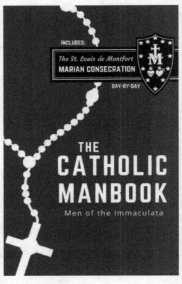

- Top Catholic Apps, Websites, and Blogs
- Everything you need to pray the Rosary
- The Most Effective Daily Prayers & Novenas, including the Emergency Novena
- Going to Confession and Eucharistic Adoration like a boss!
- Mastering the Catholic Liturgical Calendar

The Catholic ManBook contains the collective wisdom of The Men of the Immaculata, of saints, priests and laymen, fathers and sons, single and married. Holiness is at your fingertips. Get your copy today.

This edition also includes a revised and updated St. Louis de Montfort Marian consecration. Follow the prayers in a day-by-day format.

The Seventh Word

The FIRST Pro-Life Horror Novel!

Pro-Life hero, Abby Johnson, called it "legit scary ... I don't like reading this as night! ... It was good, it was so good ... it was terrifying, but good."

The First Word came with Cain, who killed the first child of man. The Third Word was Pharaoh's instruction to the midwives. The Fifth Word was carried from Herod to Bethlehem. One of the Lost Words dwelt among the Aztecs and hungered after their children.

Evil hides behind starched white masks. The ancient Aztec demon now

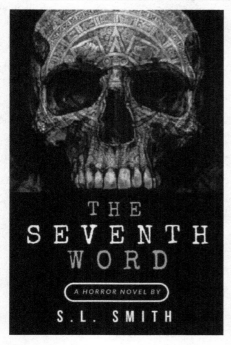

conducts his affairs in the sterile environment of corporate medical facilities. An insatiable hunger draws the demon to a sleepy Louisiana hamlet.

There, it contracts the services of a young attorney, Jim David, whose unborn child is the ultimate object of the demon's designs. Monsignor, a mysterious priest of unknown age and origin, labors unseen to save the soul of a small town hidden deep within Louisiana's plantation country, nearly forgotten in a bend of the Mississippi River.

You'll be gripped from start to heart-stopping finish in this page-turning thriller.

With roots in Bram Stoker's Dracula, this horror novel reads like Stephen King's classic stories of towns being slowly devoured by an unseen evil and the people who unite against it.

The book is set in southern Louisiana, an area the author brings to life with compelling detail based on his local knowledge.

Blessed is He Who ...
Models of Catholic Manhood

You are the average of the five people you spend the most time with, so spend more time with the Saints! Here are several men that you need to get to know whatever your age or station in life. These short biographies will give you an insight into how to live better, however you're living.

- **From Kings to computer nerds**, old married couples to single teenagers, these men gave us extraordinary examples of holiness:

- Pier Giorgio Frassati & Carlo Acutis – Here are two extraordinary **young men**, an athlete and a computer nerd, living on either side of the 20th Century

- Two men of royal stock, Francesco II and Archduke Eugen, lived lives of holiness despite all the world conspiring against them.

There's also the **simple husband and father**, Blessed Luigi. Though he wasn't a king, he can help all of us treat the women in our lives as queens.

Blessed Is He Who ... Models of Catholic Manhood explores the lives of six men who found their greatness in Christ and His Bride, the Church. In six succinct chapters, the authors, noted historian Brian J. Costello and theologian and attorney Scott L. Smith, share with you the uncommon lives of exceptional men who will one day be numbered among the Saints of Heaven, men who can bring all of us closer to sainthood.

THANKS FOR READING!
TOTUS TUUS

CPSIA information can be obtained
at www.ICGtesting.com
Printed in the USA
LVHW041531160523
747047LV00003BA/518